THE SERMONS OF MR. YORICK

THE SERMONS OF MR. YORICK

by Laurence Sterne

selected by

Marjorie David

FYFIELD BOOKS

A Carcanet Press Publication

SBN 85635 056 7—cloth
SBN 85635 057 5—paper

Copyright © Marjorie S. David 1973

First Published in 1973
by Carcanet Press Limited
266 Councillor Lane
Cheadle Hulme, Cheadle
Cheshire SK8 5PN

Printed in Great Britain
by W & J Mackay Limited, Chatham

CONTENTS

THE SERMONS OF MR. YORICK

INTRODUCTION

I.

HOMENAS who had to preach next Sunday (before God knows whom) knowing nothing at all of the matter—was all this while at it as hard as he could drive in the next room:—for having fouled two clean sheets of his own, and being quite stuck fast in the entrance upon his third general *division*, and finding himself unable to get either forwards or backwards with any grace—'Curse it,' says he, (thereby excommunicating every mother's son who should think differently) 'why may not a man lawfully call for help in this, as in any other human emergency?'—So without any more argumentation, except starting up and nimming down from the top shelf but one, the second volume of CLARK—tho' without any felonius intention of so doing, he had begun to clap me in (making a joint first) five whole pages, nine round paragraphs, and a dozen and a half of good thoughts all in a row; and because there was a confounded high gallery—was transcribing it away like a little devil.—Now—quoth HOMENAS to himself 'tho' I hold all this to be fair and square, yet, if I am found out, there will be the deuce and all to pay.'

POOR HOMENAS, in this *Extract in the Manner of Rabelais*, published posthumously by Sterne's daughter to flesh out a collection of letters, falls from his 'confounded high gallery,' paying for his homiletic forgeries with a broken neck. Sterne himself suffered no such fate, but his early life as a clergyman may be easily read into this character Homenas who, uninspired by doctrine or congregation, garnered a few rounded phrases from the most convenient volume at hand in order to fill his regular Sunday obligation. Sterne's other clerical alter-ego, Yorick, is a more original thinker. Others steal sermons from him. These two characters may be fairly said to represent Sterne at the two stages of his career. As an obscure parish priest, he churned out the requisite number of homilies without interest or imagination. Later, having 'dirtyed his frock,' as Mrs. Montague said, with *Tristram Shandy*, he became conscious of the impression any of his writing might make on the world, and the nature of his preaching changed. 'God knows whom' included such noteworthy congregants as Baron d'Holbach and David Hume; an unlikely audience, but one better suited to inspire this unlikely clergyman to rhetorical tricks and human insights as delightful as those he employed in his novels.

Sterne's adventures after the first volumes of *Tristram* appeared are fairly well known. But until that time, when he entered the literary world as an immediate success at the age of forty-six, he was deeply involved in Church life in and around York. The book that shocked and delighted London and Paris had begun as a local satire, and the events which occupied Sterne before he began his career as a novelist were as important to the nature of his later work as any that came after.

Certainly Sterne did not set out upon his vocation in the Church of England with particularly grave thoughts about religion. As a fatherless young man, his decision was one of financial expedience and had probably been made for him by relatives before he even entered Jesus College, Cambridge. The Sternes had a long tradition of Church service, and Sterne's great-grandfather, the Archbishop Richard Sterne, had been a devoted High Church loyalist during and after the civil war. At the time Laurence went up to Jesus his uncle, Dr. Jacques Sterne (described by Wilbur Cross as 'the eager pluralist'), was probably seen by Laurence's guardians as a heaven-sent path to preferment. This conjecture eventually, if temporarily, proved to be true. Jacques Sterne is not known for his overriding interest in widows and orphans, and he in fact paid no attention to his young relative until all of Laurence's college expenses were safely in the past. After that, Dr. Sterne 'discovered' his nephew, expecting him to be a valuable aide-de-camp in the political manoeuvring at York Minster, where the older man was precentor to the cathedral.

Laurence Sterne's progress through the ranks early in his career seemed nothing short of miraculous. Two months after taking his undergraduate degree Sterne was ordained deacon. By the next year, 1738, he was licensed to serve as curate at Catton, and in the same year was ordained priest. Four days after his ordination Laurence Sterne was collated to the vicarage of Sutton-

8

on-Forest. This living, worth £40 annually, was—not surprisingly —convenient to York and Uncle Jacques. Sterne immediately hired a curate and until his marriage stayed at York, close to both his powerful benefactor and the lively social atmosphere of this growing, northern trade city. In 1740–41, the prebend of Givendale was resigned by the incumbent, and young Sterne became a member of the York Chapter, preaching turns at the Cathedral on a regular basis. Another prebendal stall fell open in 1741, and Sterne resigned Givendale for this more lucrative position, the prebend of North Newbald.

Sterne's prospects by 1741 seemed promising enough for him to risk marriage with Elizabeth Lumley, whom he had courted for two years. 'She owned she liked me,' he wrote later to his daughter, 'but thought herself not rich enough, or me too poor, to be joined together—' The inducement of rejection must have made Eliza Lumley a particularly inviting challenge to Sterne, so that in spite of other peripheral love interests he pursued her with a barrage of love letters until she consented to give her hand. The young couple began refurbishing the vicarage at Sutton soon after their wedding. Some of the expense of this project was offset when Sterne was licensed pluralist, having been granted the vicarage of Stillington parish in 1743.

Settling at Sutton, with the added obligation of preaching thirteen yearly sermons at Stillington, did not lead Sterne to expend unnecessary energy upon his congregations. A story related by one of Sterne's friends had him one day walking over to Stillington to preach, probably armed with the same sermon he had used that morning at Sutton. On his way his dog flushed a flock of game birds, and Sterne calmly returned home for his gun, leaving the parishioners waiting until he had finished hunting. Sterne had little inclination to compromise, and constantly 'ran . . . foul of somebody's tackling . . .' as he describes Yorick doing in *Tristram*. He quarrelled early on with Phillip Harland, Squire of Sutton, a dedicated Tory who raised Sterne's whiggish ire. Parishioners, as was usual in such cases, took sides, most often with Harland. They had good reason to. With his characteristic thoughtlessness Sterne, making at the time several clumsy attempts at farming, undersold local farmers in butter.

If there were skirmishes in Sutton parish, however, there is no evidence that Sterne incurred lasting bitterness there. He was absent-minded and eccentric, but could be, at least at times, a dedicated vicar. Some indication of Sterne's attitude toward his work during the twenty years he spent at Sutton may be found in his answer to a questionnaire distributed by Archbishop Herring of York in preparation for his visitation in May, 1743. Sterne's answers show that he fulfilled his parish duties ably. Among other replies he notes that 'I Catechise every Sunday in my Church during Lent, But explain our Religion to the Children and Servants of my Parishioners in my own House every Sunday Night during Lent, from six o'clock till nine. I mention the Length of Time as my reason for not doing it in Church.' Canon S. L. Ollard, who found the document and published it in the *Times Literary Supplement*, 18 March, 1926, comments, 'In all the hundreds of returns which . . . I have examined this is unique and stands alone.' No other cleric among 800 queried had held three hours of instruction or confirmation class in his home for the six Sunday evenings of Lent. Sterne also showed an interest in the personal well-being of members of his flock, helping out with an easy good humour unclouded, in times of need, by moral censure. He writes of an adulteress presented at Stillington Visitation for penance: 'She is as poor as a Church Mouse & cannot absolutely raise a Shilling, To save her Life, so pray let her have the Pennance—and as far as the Stamps, I will take care of the discharge. If not above 3 or 4 Shillings—'

II.

STERNE's life as a country preacher represented only part of his activity in the Church. As a prebend at York he became involved in the more serious arguments and intrigues within the Cathedral Close. Aside from his debt to his uncle, whose power was enforced by several other titles of preferment in addition to that of precentor at York, Sterne also owed thanks to other influential men of the diocese. From the beginning Sterne had courted the favour of the archbishop, Lancelot Blackburn, and Dean Richard Osbaldeston, who licensed Sterne at Stillington and to whom the young prelate later dedicated a sermon.

Laurence Sterne's first sally into the political world as a Church partisan came in the 1741 elections which ultimately overthrew Walpole. At York the 'Court Party', favouring the status quo, may be identified with the Whigs. The 'Country Party', or the Tories, suggested reforms which seemed to offer a genuine threat to Church power. Whig and Tory members were elected to the new parliament in equal proportion from both county and city of York, but the county Whig representative died during the summer, forcing a by-election. The Tories nominated George Fox, a Leeds landowner eager for election. The Whigs fell back on Chomley Turner, a seasoned parliamentarian, but a man with no real desire to run again. Saddled with an unwilling candidate, Church partisans undertook especially careful measures to ensure his victory. The only York newspaper at the time was edited by a Tory; Jacques Sterne provided finance to begin a new paper, the *York Gazetteer*, edited by a Whig. To make sure those who only read Tory news would be exposed to the Whig point of view, Laurence Sterne was assigned to enter into an anonymous correspondence with a Tory in the opposition paper. An exchange of tasteless *ad hominem* blows ensued, and Sterne was finally unmasked as the nameless 'concerned citizen' when his handwriting was recognized. He also wrote longer articles for Dr. Sterne which appeared in the *Gazetteer*. Turner was finally elected, and Sterne's reward was the prebend of North Newbald.

In 1742, when all of this political uproar should have abated, the Whig representative for York city died. Fox stood again, but conditions were different; Walpole had fallen. The Tory was elected unanimously. Laurence Sterne, realizing the new direction politics had taken, wrote to the Tory *Courant* in his own name in July 1742 that '. . . it may not be improper to change sides . . . I sincerely beg Pardon for the abusive Gazetteers I wrote during the late contested Election for the County of York, and . . . I heartily wish Mr. Fox Joy of his Election for the City.' This sporting reply was not likely to have pleased the ever-bitter Dr. Sterne, who never took his losses lightly. It is probable that uncle and nephew were at odds even at this time. Laurence Sterne was already resisting the menial task of pamphletting and letter-writing for his uncle, thinking such dirty-work beneath him. In addition it was

11

rumoured that Laurence had encroached with open impunity on his uncle's mistress, no way to patch up an ailing friendship.

Personal difficulties, however, were temporarily forgotten in the face of a real national threat. In 1743 Archbishop Herring succeeded Archbishop Blackburn, and the Sternes joined with him in preparation for York's defence during the Jacobite insurrection of 1745. York Minster watched with horror as the Stuarts advanced as far as Derbyshire, and churchmen participated actively in arming the city against possible attack. Herring preached with passion in defence of his Majesty. It is probable that Sterne wrote in his uncle's behalf again, contributing to the local successor of the *Gazetteer* and London periodicals as well. The eventual rout of the Stuarts was a victory, according to the loyal archbishop, against 'Popery and Arbitrary Power under a French and Spanish Government'. Taking a cue from this exalted rhetoric, Dr. Jacques Sterne seized the opportunity for several acts of zealotry astounding in their disregard for the world as it was. He attempted to revive laws from the time of Elizabeth and of William against hearing Mass, proselytizing and Roman Catholic schools. His principal victims in this particular project were two old women who conducted a Catholic school for girls at York. Dr. Sterne initiated an essentially groundless lawsuit against 'the Popish Nunnery' which dragged through the courts until 1751, when the case was finally dropped. He also took the victory as a chance to cause difficulties for a long time adversary, the Tory Dr. John Burton, immortal today more because of Laurence Sterne's caricature of him as 'the squat, uncourtly figure' Dr. Slop than for his actual praiseworthy work in obstetrics.

Burton first drew the malice of the Sternes during the 1741 by-elections, when he electioneered vigorously for his Tory candidate. After this he was subjected to minor harassments by Dr. Sterne and his friends, most of which he overcame, successfully continuing his medical research and practice. But in 1745 Dr. Burton posted west to North Riding to look after his estates there, fearing that the Highlanders would pass through. The Stuarts took another route, but seized Dr. Burton himself at Hornby in North Riding, and conveyed him to Lancaster, finally releasing him with a safe-conduct pass to return home. Arriving at York he was brought before Dr. Sterne and another magistrate, and found himself detained at York castle as 'a suspicious person to his Majesty's Government'.

During this imprisonment Dr. Sterne published several defaming letters in a local newspaper, accusing Burton of collusion in his own capture. Burton applied for bail, but this was denied him; Dr. Sterne claimed that new evidence would be produced proving the doctor guilty of high treason. Fortunately, before Burton could be tried and executed, the secretary of state called for the prisoner in order to examine him before the Privy Council in London. After an entire year's detention, Burton was released, and he eventually regained his position in York. He published several books, including *An Essay Toward a Complete New System of Midwifery*, which Laurence Sterne parodied in *Tristram Shandy*. The younger Sterne's hatred of Burton was almost as intense as that of his uncle. Burton was locally known for indiscretion, haughtiness and outspokenness. It seems likely, in fact, that Sterne selected him for caricature more for bad manners than bad politics. Sterne had also read the midwifery tract and found it ridiculous; as a pedant and philistine, Burton struck Sterne as a logical figure of fun.

This does not excuse the actual persecutions to which Burton was subjected. Laurence Sterne did at that time have a provincial hatred of Catholicism. Burton was a Papist. Sterne was also morally and emotionally distressed by the Inquisition, to which he returns continually both in fiction and in various sermons. Not until Sterne travelled to France and Italy and saw Catholics leading normal, happy lives did he understand that existence could be decent under the auspices of Rome.

There was some diocesan office-shuffling after the Highlanders' revolt. Archbishop Herring was translated to the see of Canterbury and replaced by Matthew Hutton. Richard Osbaldeston was elevated to the bishopric of Carlisle and succeeded by John Fontayne, a college friend of Laurence Sterne's. Jacques Sterne was passed over for preferment, probably because of a rebuke he received from the secretary of state for his Dr. Burton campaign and other similar incidents. Laurence Sterne received some minor marks of honour but no real preferment. Squabbles had been revived in this time of national peace. Archbishop Hutton and Dr. Sterne, men of similar doctrine and the same generation, allied themselves with like-minded conservative churchmen. Dean Fontayne, with Laurence Sterne and other younger, liberal canons, formed another faction.

The bitterness which had first separated Sterne from his uncle grew worse with time. Counting on the protection of his influential new friends, he probably refused the role of subordinate adamantly. The angry Dr. Sterne tried to drive his 'ungrateful and unworthy nephew' from York, and Sterne's own quick temper gave him and his friends few opportunities to placate the older man. An argument arose over Sterne's preaching turns for absent clergymen at the Cathedral. This was a source of extra income for young members of the chapter, and Dr. Sterne had no qualms about cutting his nephew off from the source. Young Sterne did have powerful allies, however, and it seemed for a while as if he would retain his position in spite of his uncle's wrath. There was, however, a useful issue at hand which could be used to keep Laurence Sterne from spending too much time at York.

Agnes Sterne, Laurence's mother, had come to England from Ireland in 1742, having heard that her son had married a great heiress. Sterne's efforts to dispel this illusion had no effect, and Agnes, with her daughter Catherine, stayed at Chester until 1747 when they moved to York to be near Laurence's tremendous wealth. Sterne suggested several alternative plans after finding that his mother refused to return to Ireland and her widow's pension. He offered an allowance, which was refused as too small. He tried to place his sister as a lady's companion or, if she wished to keep herself, to help finance a shop for her. Both suggestions were refused as unworthy of a woman of gentle birth. Meanwhile Sterne and his wife contributed money toward the support of the two women. Sterne claimed in a letter to his uncle that he gave all that he had to spare, which may or may not be true. He was not, in any case, a wealthy man. There is evidence as well that his marital situation was already deteriorating, and it could be for this reason that he did not take his mother and sister into his own home; it is also possible that Sterne and his mother had never got along. Settlement of some kind could have been made in time, but impatient Agnes sent Catherine to appeal to Jacques Sterne. He was more than happy to take up their case. Dean Fontayne, hearing of this, attempted to effect a reconciliation between uncle and nephew with the younger Sterne's consent. Dr. Sterne refused the offer, and three months later had Agnes and Catherine placed in some charitable institution, either public workhouse or 'common gaol', spreading the story that Laurence Sterne was responsible.

The women were, as opposed to the popular story to the contrary, eventually released, but Sterne had lost the war with his uncle. He spent more time at Sutton and began farming again, devoting himself to friends, hunting, painting and reading. Bad weather, local problems and his daughter's poor health, about which Sterne was deeply concerned, increased his isolation. Except during harvest season Sterne managed to go to York once a week, and he still took his turns preaching at the minster. Generally, however, he withdrew from Church politics. His mother accepted the proffered allowance and reconciliation followed. Late in 1748, however, bored with farming and land deals, Sterne rid himself of most of his parish business, entrusting most of it to his curate, and rented his lands. At this time he made one, final venture into Church disputes, an act which was to determine the course of the rest of his life.

Apparently many of the smaller quarrels between dean and archbishop at York were fomented by a Dr. Francis Topham (Didius in *Tristram Shandy*), a lawyer whose collection of diocesan advisory positions and commisaryships rivalled Dr. Sterne's titles of preferment. Topham had amassed a personal fortune as early as 1751, but in that year the Commissaryship of the Peculiar Court of Pickering and Pocklington, to be assigned at the discretion of the dean, fell open. Topham tried to secure this office (which was actually worth very little), and had earlier obtained the verbal promise of it from Dean Fontayne. The dean, however, became disillusioned with the lawyer and made another, temporary arrangement with Topham's consent, thought himself rid of Topham and finally granted the office to Laurence Sterne. This particularly angered Topham, who spread the rumour that the dean had broken his word. Dean Fontayne, Sterne and a few other of their allies confronted the lawyer with his stories at a dinner party and apparently shamed him into a disavowal. After this, Topham made a point of ingratiating himself with the archbishop at the dean's

15

expense. In 1757 Archbishop Hutton left York for Canterbury and was replaced by Dr. John Gilbert, a man suffering from chronic ill health. Archbishop Gilbert quickly became dependent upon his advisor, Topham, who spared no pains to be of special use. The lawyer was solicitous and efficient, so that when he made a special request of the archbishop in 1758, Dr. Gilbert readily consented. Topham had discovered an archaic law applicable to his patent as Commissary of the Exchequer and Prerogative Courts, which granted the position for two lives rather than one. He wished in his son's interest that the patent be opened and this old clause added to it. The transaction, however, could not go through without the consent of the dean and Chapter as well as the archbishop; even after conciliatory letters from the lawyer to Dean Fontayne his request was turned down. Topham decided to appeal to the public with a sixpenny pamphlet in which he brought up the denial of the Pickering and Pocklington post and all the trivial bickerings of the past ten years. The dean replied with his own pamphlet, which included signed testimony from Laurence Sterne and other justices of the peace as to what took place at the dinner party in 1741. Topham replied to the reply, insinuating that the dean's entire pamphlet had been written by other people. In late January 1759, just after the issue of Topham's last pamphlet, Laurence Sterne prepared another publication, entitled *A Political Romance*, in which York was reduced to a country parish with Topham portrayed as 'Trim the dogcatcher', a niggling cheat who wished to acquire 'a good, warm watchcoat', which had actually been designated for other, better purposes. The manuscript included a *Key* in which members of the parish political club, also caricatures of local figures (including Sterne, who appears in *Political Romance* as well), were shown discussing the 'true meaning' of the story which had gone before. The burlesque was skillfully wrought and Sterne, proud of his creation, signed the work, included an open letter to Topham, demanded a higher price for it than the ordinary pamphlet brought, and saw it through the press. It was a revelation of Sterne's true *metier*. Satirical, insinuating, boisterous and irreverant, it surpassed any of Sterne's previous attempts at 'witty' poetry or his bawdy letters written to discredit political opponents. The trouble was that *Political Romance* was utterly devastating. Immedi-

16

ately on publication Topham offered to quit all claims if it were only suppressed. Sterne's friends, too, were embarrassed by the effort. Although archbishop and dean were treated with all due kindness, they were being laughed at nonetheless. The work detracted from the dignity of the Church, and with the annoying Topham so quickly vanquished, unsold copies were bought up and burned.

Political Romance and the scandal which attended it brought Sterne a great deal of public attention. Its suppression also hurt his pride. He began writing *Tristram Shandy* that year, and said in a letter to a Mrs. F. 'Now for your desire of knowing the reason for my turning author? Why truly I am tired of employing my brains for other people's advancement.' In 1760 Sterne moved from Sutton to his beloved Shandy Hall. After the novel's sudden success, his occasional preaching and all his writing was done as much in his capacity as a novelist as that of churchman, for no one's benefit but his own.

III.

REPORTS from Sterne's contemporaries about his preaching style vary. On one hand John Croft remembers 'half the congregation' walking out when Yorick took the pulpit at York minster; others apparently found his style delightful. Legend has it that Sterne, on the morning after his wedding, chose to expound upon the text 'we have toiled all night and have taken nothing'. There must have been at least an element of curiosity bringing congregants to church on Sunday. It is likely that Sterne's weak lungs did not lead to the possession of a strong speaking voice, but he was known to love talking and oration; he was deeply conscious of the best way to deliver a verbal message, and dwells long and artfully on Trim's voice cadence, body position and gesture when he delivers Yorick's sermon in *Tristram Shandy*. Sterne liked the sermon's potential for drama, but preaching itself did not appeal to him as a form. Thinking of Swift's Laputia, he wrote to a friend, 'preaching (as you must know) is a theologic flap upon the heart, as the dunning for a promise is a political flap upon the memory:—both the one and the other is useless where men have *wit enough* to be honest.' He made

17

his messages brief, wishing not to fatigue '. . . myself and my flock to death—' Sterne's love of jest, though, and his inability to exclude himself from among those he observed and commented on, made his best sermons anything but fatiguing for his congregants.

Sterne's doctrinal message is unoriginal most of the time. The strength of his preaching rests on his clear depiction of familiar types, his penetrating observations of human nature. Jesus answers the lawyer's question about who is his neighbour, for instance, '. . . not by any far-fetch'd refinement from the schools of the Rabbis, which might sooner have silenced than convinced the man— but by a direct appeal to human nature in the instance he relates of a man falling amongst thieves . . .' or, in 'Self Knowledge', David responds to Nathan's tale because '. . . the whole was so tenderly addressed to the heart and passions, as to kindle at once the utmost horror and indignation'.

It follows from this that Sterne was influenced in his homiletic writing more by the philosopher Locke than by any theologian. Sterne's implicit assertion that man becomes bored or uneasy when not confronted with new sensations, or when he fails to renew old ones, may be inferred from Locke and informs all of Sterne's work. That Sterne transformed this idea into a writing style which is temporally discontinuous and thematically varied is an act of creative imagination, but it is perhaps not unfair to assert that Locke, more than anyone else, gave Sterne the confidence to use the idiosyncratic style for which he became famous. Certainly Sterne was not writing from theory; his influences were manifold and various. From the early sermons, however, it is evident that he did not write successfully unless his wandering sensibility was given free play. Locke's implied approval of this must have meant a great deal to the author. His influence is to be found among the sermons specifically in 'The Prodigal Son' where Sterne adapts ideas from *Thoughts Concerning Education* for his summation, which discusses the merits and dangers of 'the grand tour'. He adopts Locke's own examples in some cases, illustrating and expanding the subject with his familiar humour and attention to detail. In the context of the earlier part of the sermon, this conclusion is not surprising. The Prodigal is described in terms which would have been familiar to the parents of any son who had 'done the continent'. '. . . he was cheated at Damascus by one of the best men in the world; . . . he had lent a part of his substance to a friend at Nineveh, who had fled off with it to the Ganges; . . . a whore of Babylon had swallowed his best pearl . . .' Making exotic subjects familiar was one of Sterne's favourite homiletic devices. Locke, who was more a contemporary spokesman than an explicator of the past, had a logical appeal for Sterne. That his ideas influenced Sterne's religious writings was also in keeping with Yorick's high opinion of the philosopher. He wrote to a friend that Locke's thought was 'a sacred philosophy, which the world must heed if it is to have a true science of morals, and which man must heed also if he is to gain real command over nature'.

At the same time, Sterne's personal beliefs conformed to the creed of the Church. He was not a deist, and mentioned frequently the evidences of Holy Religion, though he declined to discuss them any further. He took the Church and its teachings for granted, and apparently cared little for issues of historical christianity. In this he was very much a man of his time. He was not an 'enthusiast'; preaching common sense and good taste he preached, in terms of the age in which he lived, good morality.

As publications, the seven books of sermons were highly successful in their time. Volumes I and II, published in the wake of the first great sensation of *Tristram Shandy*, boasted 661 subscribers and immediately went into new editions (*Sentimental Journey*, which became a popular success after publication, had a quarter that number of initial subscribers). Of volumes III and IV Sterne wrote '. . . it goes into the world with a prancing list *de tout noblesse*—which will bring me three hundred pounds, exclusive of the sale of copy'. The three final volumes, compiled after Sterne's death, were also popular. Aside from one reviewer who initially took umbrage at religious writing appearing under the facetious name 'Mr. Yorick', the volumes were generally well received by press as well as public, and were included on several lists of recommended reading for young ladies. Sterne claimed that he published the sermons to balance his 'shandaic character'; he had been warned by prudent friends that the publication of *Tristram* might block his chances for preferment. 'But suppose preferment is long a coming,' he complained in a letter to Rev. John Blake, who advised him to get preferment first, then write anything he pleased, '(and for aught I know I may not be preferred till the Resurrection of the Just) an am all that time in labour—how must I bear my Pains? —' Sterne went ahead with his novel but included, in his original publisher's contract, a clause providing for two books of sermons. Financially, this arrangement was prudent for both Sterne and his publisher. Sermons were respectable reading at the time, and any cleric who produced a few volumes was bound to profit.

The poet Gray wrote to Thomas Wharton in 1760 that the sermons '. . . shew a very strong imagination and a sensible heart: but you see him often tottering in the verge of laughter, and ready to throw his perriwig in the face of the audience'. Christianity's message of joy was the one which Sterne most successfully conveyed. In 'The Prodigal Son' he tells his congregation that 'When the affections so kindly break loose, Joy, is another name for Religion'. Joy itself, he believed, was a way to religious understanding. Sterne sublimely conveys this idea in *Sentimental Journey*, when after dining with a peasant family Yorick's hosts begin to sing and dance: '. . . I could distinguish an elevation of spirit different from that which is the cause or the effect of simple jollity.—In a word, I thought I beheld *Religion* mixing in the dance . . .' The narrator doubts the truth of his feeling, but it is confirmed when the old man of the family tells him '. . . that all his life long he had made it a rule, after supper was over, to call out his family to dance and rejoice; believing, he said, that a cheerful and contented mind was the best sort of thanks to heaven that an illiterate peasant could pay—

—or a learned prelate either, said I.'

From this attitude one wonders to what extent Sterne's invocation against the House of Feasting was delivered with tongue in cheek. Sterne probably meant his preaching to be, like 'true shandyism', against nothing except 'spleen'. If Sterne did not burst into laughter and throw his perriwig into his congregants' laps, he did make them laugh. In 'Self Knowledge' he suggests that man is the worst casuist when called upon to judge himself, '. . . that dearest of all parties—so closely connected with him—so much and so long beloved—of whom he has so early conceived the highest opinion and esteem, and with whose merit he has all along, no doubt, found so much reason to be contented'. In speech, he could employ the dramatic dash with at least as great effect for comedy or surprise as he did on the printed page. He says of Solomon in 'The Levite': 'this was remarkable in that [case] of Solomon, whose excess became an insult upon the privileges of mankind; for by the same plan of luxury, which made it necessary to have forty thousand stalls of horses—he had unfortunately miscalculated his other wants, and so had seven hundred wives, and three hundred concubines.

'Wise—deluded man! was it not that thou madest some amends for thy practice with thy good preaching, what had become of thee! —three hundred—but let us turn aside, I beseech you, from so sad a stumbling block.'

Certainly the sermons contain many of the features which contribute to the appeal of Sterne's fiction. They use the device of internal monologue, create lively, recognizable characters, digress from the point to an interesting side issue and manipulate the reader to laughter, surprise, or in his own time, tears. His sermon style is often as subtle and flexible as that which intrigued the first readers of his novels.

As is usual with Sterne, he does not dwell on buildings and landscapes in the sermons. His settings for action are akin to stage sets, presented and then left the same for the course of the discussion. Yorick concentrates on his living characters, and rather than move them from place to place he often condenses whole years of a person's life into a list. The man of fashion, inquiring after happiness, '—drops all gainful pursuits—withdraws himself from the busy part of the world—realizes—pulls down—builds up again. Buys statues, pictures—plants—and plucks up by the roots—levels mountains—and fills up vallies—turns rivers into dry ground, and dry ground into rivers . . .' This technique is in itself Biblical, and Sterne quotes directly from the Bible when he describes the long series of luxurious foods which grace Solomon's table in 'The Rich Man and Lazarus'. The sermons are filled with lists—strings of misfortunes, parades of wives and concubines, numbers of household treasures. That Sterne learned this method from the Bible is likely. It was a book to which he referred continually in all his writing.

The Bible itself, however, was not enough for Sterne in terms of the material it provided for preaching. Since he derided teleological controversy as pedantic, Yorick found that the best way to make his point was to expand upon the Biblical stories and passages he chose for subjects. In almost every sermon, he beseeches his audience to allow him to extend the parable, that a lesson might be better drawn. In this way Hezekiah is left to consider for several paragraphs his death and the bad results which might derive from it. He ends by making a kind of bargain with God, though Sterne probably did not mean to imply that this was the case. The Levite whose concubine has run away spends a good deal of time dwelling on sweet memories of love, and the advantages of charity toward the penitent. Sterne adds the internal conflict that the Bible does not consider. In this way, though he takes liberties with the text, he employs it to appeal to the sensibility, molding and reshaping the Bible to accommodate the issues he finds most important. Through this process he enters into the Biblical character's manner of reasoning. 'The Holy man knew,' he says of Nathan, 'that was it any one's case but David's own, no man would have been so quick-sighted in discerning the nature of the injury.' The vicar in Sterne was always giving way to the writer's need to make fiction of fact, in order to render reality meaningful. This deep care for motive is one which appeals to present day readers, heirs to Freud, and makes the sermons easier going as theology today than they might have been in the past. Generally, however, Sterne met with little complaint in his own time about his liberality with the Bible. More important to his flock was the message he preached, and this in no way transgressed on society's structure or prerogatives. The rich man who denies Lazarus crumbs from his table is not denied heaven because of his wealth, but because he misuses it. '. . . the case might be then, as now: his quality and station in the world might have been supposed to be such, as not only to have justified his doing this [living lavishly] but, in general, to have required it without any imputation of doing wrong; for differences of station there must be in the world, which must be supported by such marks of distinction as custom imposes.' Sterne was no friend of miserliness, and his chief subject for discourse was charity, but as long as he did not indulge in a Wesleyan inclination for 'raving' his foibles might be taken in stride. No matter how unusual his form, his message was always acceptable to polite society.

Although Sterne freely elaborates the characters in his homilies, his constraint in the sermon is often evident in other ways. There are instances in the novels where Yorick's wry perception of human nature would not have been suited to the pulpit. After Bobby dies in *Tristram Shandy* the effects of the loss echo through the house— but very little of the stir the incident causes involves distress over the loss of a son. The servants at Shandy Hall lament the passing of such things as madam's green satin night-gown, and are brought to tears only by the ever dramatic Trim and his skilled dropping of a hat. Walter Shandy, after the usual consultation of the Ancients, turns to the pursuit of educating Tristram, his last and dubious hope. In 'The House of Mourning' Sterne says that when entering a bereaved home, one could not 'insult the unfortunate even with an improper look—under what levity or dissipation of heart.' Sterne, however, knew better, and himself had trouble summoning the 'serious and devout frame of mind' which he claims certain situations demand. His gravity was limited by his acute instinct to observe, search the heart, and realize the ironic contradictions that lay therein. For this reason the sermons cannot be considered the literary equals of the novels. Yorick was limited by the form and, regardless of the freedoms he took in spite of this, he was preaching to a real congregation and could not do with the subjects at hand what his personality usually demanded. Because of this one perceives the restrained quality of many of the sermons: 'The Rich Man and Lazarus', probably one of Sterne's better early efforts, adheres most closely to accepted homiletic style and is in consequence highly derivative. Sterne had not a creative theological mind. Like Homenas, he was not averse to nimming down a book of published sermons from the shelf and transcribing away. Later, when he used the homily as a creative form in other instances, this 'borrowing' became infrequent.

When Sterne brought his emotions to a subject, for example, its meaning was affectingly conveyed. 'Consider slavery—what it is— how bitter a draught, and how many millions have been made to drink of it;—which if it can poison all earthly happiness when exercised barely upon our bodies, what must it be, when it comprehends slavery of both body and mind? . . . examine the prisons of the inquisition, hear the melancholy notes sounded in every cell

. . . the exquisite tortures . . . mercilessly inflicted on the un-fortunate, where the racked and weary soul has so often wished to take its leave,—but cruelly suffered not to depart.' This digression in 'Job' echoes one in the 'Abuses of Conscience' which Trim reads aloud in *Tristram*. There is little doubt that Sterne's own feelings about slavery were strong. He was aware as well that to certain others such human distress could pass without notice. Trim inter-rupts the sermon to remember his brother, a victim of the inquisi-tion: '(Oh! 'tis my brother, cried poor *Trim* in a most passionate exclamation, dropping the sermon upon the ground, and clapping his hands together . . . —Why *Trim*, said my father, this is not a history,—'tis a sermon thou art reading; prithee begin the sentence again.)' The fact that his listeners would probably leave church thinking "tis only a sermon' could not have failed to annoy Sterne. He clearly believed that his message, joyous or sad, could reach people better through his fiction than through his turns in the pulpit. He wrote to Ignatius Sancho, a freed slave who admired Sterne and begged him to remember the oppressed, 'If I can weave the Tale I have wrote [about a poor slave girl] into the Work I'm abt—tis at the service of the afflicted . . . it casts a sad Shade upon the World.' In *Sentimental Journey* Sterne's famous passage about the caged starling and the personal fear of slavery the bird inspires in Yorick shows that he had not forgotten the issue of slavery or his promise to Sancho.

Sterne also discoursed on one of his favourite subjects in the passage taken from *Genesis* for 'The Levite and his Concubine', where he reflects that 'it is not good for man to be alone', leaving 'the torpid monk' to seek heaven comfortless. In *Sentimental Journey* he is prompted to use almost the same words '—Surely—Surely man! it is not good for thee to sit alone—' and later, 'If nature has so wove her web of kindness, that some threads of love and desire are entangled with the piece—must the whole web be rent in drawing them out?—Whip me such stoics, great governor of nature!' The particular kind of humorous emotional excess which allows Yorick to ask God to whip stoics could obviously not be exercised in a sermon. But Sterne conveys his message nevertheless in 'The Levite', even including an invocation against prudery. In this lament he might also be considered to address himself to those nineteenth century moral guardians who attempted to bury his whole *oeuvre* under a mound of personal condemnation. Sterne, no 'torpid monk', involved himself in several real or imagined entanglements with women throughout his life. That he was unworthy to sermonize was a familiar statement. This attitude has probably still, to some extent, prevented the sermons from receiving the attention they deserve. The present age is more tolerant, but residually affected by Victorian prudery. Like Solomon, however, Sterne might be considered to have made amends for his practice with good preaching. His sermons show that he was as capable of as much sense as sensibility.

The purpose of this volume is to provide a sample of Sterne's best sermons or those which might most easily be considered relevant to the study of his formation and style as a novelist. They are therefore all drawn from Volumes I–IV. 'The Abuses of Conscience Considered' was included in Volume IV as Sermon XII, but since it is an integral part of *Tristram Shandy* there is no real point in reprinting it here. Volumes V–VII were published posthumously by Sterne's wife and daughter and constitute what Sterne referred to in a letter as 'the sweepings of the Author's study after his death'. It has been convincingly proposed that these were Sterne's earliest homilies. They are largely derivative of other theologians. It seemed wisest to include sermons only from those volumes which Sterne himself prepared for publication. Where possible, the date of delivery of a sermon has been indicated in a footnote. Speculation that all the sermons were composed before 1750 is plausible but unproven, and for further discussion of the dating of the sermons the reader is referred to *Laurence Sterne's Sermons of Mr. Yorick*, listed in the bibliography. Generally, however, there is no way to ascertain when the sermons were written or how much revision Sterne subjected them to before publication.

Marjorie S. David
Oxford. March, 1973.

TEXTUAL AND BIBLIOGRAPHICAL NOTE

Sections I and II of the Introduction to this edition of the *Sermons* rely largely on Wilbur Cross' *Life and Times of Laurence Sterne*, New Haven (1929). To date, this remains the most authoritative scholarly biography of Sterne. Quotations from Sterne's letters are taken from Lewis Perry Curtis' *Letters of Laurence Sterne*, Oxford (1935). The excellent notes to this volume comprise a full biographical picture of Sterne and his contemporaries.

The text of the sermons is based on that of the earliest available volumes; in the case of those sermons from Vol. I and II, Dodsley, London (1760) and of Vols. III and IV, Beckett and de Hondt, London (1766). Other texts have been consulted, including the Stratford-on-Avon edition of the complete sermons (1927). Sterne's spelling has been retained throughout, and editorial correction extends only to obvious printers' errors. (*) in the text indicates Sterne's own footnote.

Further Selected Bibliography:

Laurence Sterne's Sermons of Mr. Yorick, by Lansing van der Heyden Hammond; New Haven (1948)—includes a full appendix of Sterne's assorted 'borrowings' and a plausible theory about the dating of the sermons.

The Politicks of Laurence Sterne, by Lewis Perry Curtis; Oxford (1929)—a complete discussion of Sterne's political adventures while at York.

Wild Excursions: The Life and Fiction of Laurence Sterne, by David Thomson; London (1972)—the best popular biography of Sterne to date; a little hard on the famous sensibility, but generally perceptive and informative.

The Winged Skull: Papers From the Laurence Sterne Bicentenary Conference, ed. Arthur H. Cash and John M. Stedmond; London (1971)—an excellent selection of articles about Sterne from contemporary scholars.

There are several editions of *Tristram Shandy* and *Sentimental Journey*, diverse enough in binding and price to suit any inclination. *Journal to Eliza* and *Political Romance* are included with *Sentimental Journey*, however, in a paperback edition edited by Ian Jack; Oxford (1972).

Acknowledgements

For technical assistance and encouragement the editor wishes to thank James Atlas, Robert Sean Wilentz, Wayne T. Snodgrass, Roger Garfitt and Priscilla Eckhard.

1713	(24 November) Born at Clonmel, Tipperary to Ensign Roger and Agnes (?) Herbert Sterne.
1723	(or 1724) Placed in school at Halifax under the guardian-ship of father's nephew, Richard Sterne.
1731	Roger Sterne dies in West Indies, weakened by effects of a duel, 'the quarrel begun about a goose'.
1733	Enters Jesus College, Cambridge as a sizar.
1735	Matriculates at Jesus.
1736/37	receives BA.
1737/38	Ordained assistant curate at parish church of Catton, near York. Ordained 20 August, 1738 and takes over vicarage at Sutton-on-the-Forest.
1740	MA.
1741	(30 March) marries Elizabeth Lumley, cousin of Mrs. Montague.
1743	(July) 'The Unknown World' (*Gentlemen's Magazine*).
1747	*The Case of Elijah and the Widow of Zarephath Considered: A Charity Sermon*; (1 December) birth of Lydia, only surviving child.
1750	*The Abuses of Conscience Considered: A Sermon.*
1759	(January) *A Political Romance*; (December), *Tristram Shandy* vols. I and II.
1760	*The Sermons of Mr. Yorick*, vols. I and II.; moves to Coxwold.
1761	(January) *Tristram Shandy*, vols. III and IV; (December), vols. V and VI.
1762	travels to Paris, then Southern France.
1764	(May) returns to England.
1765	(January) *Tristram Shandy*, vols. VII and VIII; (October) eight months travel in France and Italy.
1766	(January) *Sermons*, vols. III and IV.
1767	(January) *Tristram Shandy*, vol. IX; meets Eliza Draper;

(March) Mrs. Draper sails for India; works on *Journal to Eliza*.

1768   (February) *A Sentimental Journey*; (18 March) Sterne dies in London.

1769   posthumous publication of *Sermons*, vols. V, VI, VII.

Sterne's Preface to the First Two Volumes of
THE SERMONS OF MR. YORICK

The Sermon which gave rise to the publication of these, having been offer'd to the world as a sermon of *Yorick's,* I hope the most serious reader will find nothing to offend him, in my continuing these volumes under the same title: lest it should be otherwise, I have added a second title page with the real name of the Author:—the first will serve the bookseller's purpose, as *Yorick's* name is possibly of the two the more known;—and the second will ease the minds of those who see a jest, and the danger which lurks under it, where no jest was meant.

I suppose it is needless to inform the Publick, that the reason of printing these sermons, arises altogether from the favourable reception, which the sermon given as a sample of them in *Tristram Shandy,* met with from the world;[1]—That sermon was printed by itself some years ago, but could find neither purchasers or readers, so that I apprehended little hazard from a promise I made upon its republication, 'That if the sermon was liked, these should be also at the world's service'; which, to be as good as my word, they here are, and I pray to GOD, they may do the service I wish it. I have little to say in their behalf, except this, that not one of them was composed with any thoughts of being printed,—they have been hastily wrote, and carry marks of it along with them.—This may be no recommendation;—I mean it however as such; for as the sermons turn chiefly upon philanthropy, and those kindred virtues to it, upon which hang all the law and the prophets, I trust they will be no less felt, or worse received, for the evidence they bear, of

---

[1] 'Abuses of Conscience'.

proceeding more from the heart than the head. I have nothing to add, but that the reader, upon old and beaten subjects, must not look for many new thoughts—'tis well if he has new language; in three or four passages, where he has neither the one or the other, I have quoted the author I made free with—there are some other passages, where I suspect I may have taken the same liberty,— but 'tis only suspicion, for I do not remember it is so, otherwise I should have restored them to their proper owners, so that I put it in here more as a general saving, than from a consciousness of having much to answer for upon that score: in this however, and every thing else, which I offer, or shall offer to the world, I rest, with a heart much at ease, upon the protection of the humane and candid, from whom I have received many favours, for which I beg leave to return them thanks——thanks.—

Sermon I
INQUIRY AFTER HAPPINESS

Psalm IV. 5, 6.
There be many that say, Who will shew us any good?—Lord lift thou up the light of thy countenance upon us.

THE GREAT pursuit of man is after happiness: it is the first and strongest desire in his nature;—in every stage of his life, he searches for it, as for hid treasure;—courts it under a thousand different shapes,—and though perpetually disappointed,—still persists—runs after and enquires for it afresh—asks every passenger who comes in his way, *Who will shew him any good?*—who will assist him in the attainment of it, or direct him to the discovery of this great end of all his wishes?

He is told by one, to search for it among the more gay and youthful pleasures of life, in scenes of mirth and sprightliness where happiness ever presides, and is ever to be known by the joy and laughter which he will see, at once painted in her looks.

A second, with a graver aspect, points out to the costly dwellings which pride and extravagance have erected:—tells the enquirer that the object he is in search of inhabits there;—that happiness lives only in company with the great, in the midst of much pomp and outward state. That he will easily find her out by the coat of many colours she has on, and the great luxury and expense of equipage and furniture with which she always sits surrounded.

The miser blesses GOD!—wonders how any one would mislead, and wilfully put him upon so wrong a scent—convinces him that happiness and extravagance never inhabited under the same roof;

—that if he would not be disappointed in his search, he must look into the plain and thrifty dwelling of the prudent man, who knows and understands the worth of money, and cautiously lays it up against an evil hour: that it is not the prostitution of wealth upon the passions, or the parting with it at all, that constitutes happiness —but that it is the keeping it together, and the *having* and *holding* it fast to him and his heirs for ever, which are the chief attributes that form this great idol of human worship to which so much incense is offered up every day.

The epicure, though he easily rectifies so gross a mistake, yet at the same time he plunges him, if possible, into a greater; for, hearing the object of his pursuit to be happiness, and knowing no other happiness than what is seated immediately in his senses—he sends the enquirer there; tells him 'tis in vain to search elsewhere for it, than where nature herself has placed it,—in the indulgence and gratification of the appetites which are given us for that end: and in a word—if he will not take his opinion in the matter—he may trust the word of a much wiser man who has assured us—that there is nothing better in this world, than that a man should eat and drink and rejoice in his works, and make his soul enjoy good in his labour —for that is his portion.

To rescue him from this brutal experiment—ambition takes him by the hand and carries him into the world,—shews him all the kingdoms of the earth and the glory of them,—points out the many ways of advancing his fortune and raising himself to honour,— lays before his eyes all the charms and bewitching temptations of power, and asks if there can be any happiness in this world like that of being caressed, courted, flattered, and followed?

To close all, the philosopher meets him bustling in full career of this pursuit—stops him—tells him, if he is in search of happiness, he is far gone out of his way.

That this deity has long been banished from noise and tumults, where there was no rest found for her, and was fled into solitude far from all commerce of the world; and in a word, if he would find her, he must leave this busy and intriguing scene, and go back to that peaceful scene of retirement and books, from which he first set out.

In this circle too often does a man run, tries all experiments, and generally sits down wearied and dissatisfied with them all at last—

in utter despair of ever accomplishing what he wants—nor knowing what to trust to after so many disappointments; or where to lay the fault, whether in the incapacity of his own nature, or the insufficiency of the enjoyments themselves.

In this uncertain and perplexed state—without knowledge which way to turn or where to betake ourselves for refuge—so often abused and deceived by the many who pretend thus to shew us any good—— Lord! says the psalmist, Lift up the light of thy countenance upon us. Send us some rays of thy grace and heavenly wisdom, in this benighted search after happiness, to direct us safely to it. O God! let us not wander for ever without a guide in this dark region in endless pursuit of our mistaken good, but enlighten our eyes that we sleep not in death—open to them the comforts of thy holy word and religion—lift up the light of thy countenance upon us,—and make us know the joy and satisfaction of living in the true faith and fear of Thee, which only can carry us to this haven of rest where we would be—that sure haven, where true joys are to be found, which will at length not only answer all our expectations—but satisfy the most unbounded of our wishes for ever and ever.

The words thus opened, naturally reduce the remaining part of the discourse under two heads.—The first part of the verse—there be many that say, Who will shew us any good?—To make some reflections upon the insufficiency of most of our enjoyments towards the attainment of happiness, upon some of the most received plans on which 'tis generally sought.

The examination of which will lead us up to the source, and the true secret of all happiness, suggested to us in the latter part of the verse—Lord! lift thou up the light of thy countenance upon us— that there can be no real happiness without religion and virtue, and the assistance of God's Grace and Holy Spirit to direct our lives in the true pursuit of it.

Let us enquire into the Disappointments of human happiness, on some of the most received plans on which 'tis generally sought for and expected, by the bulk of mankind.

There is hardly any subject more exhausted, or which at one time or other has afforded more matter for argument and declamation, than this one, of the insufficiency of our enjoyment. Scarce a reformed sensualist from Solomon down to our own days, who has not in some fits of repentance or disappointment uttered some sharp reflection upon the emptiness of human pleasure, and of the vanity of vanities which discovers itself in all the pursuits of mortal man.— But the mischief has been, that though so many good things have been said, they have generally had the fate to be considered either as the overflowings of disgust from sated appetites which could no longer relish the pleasures of life, or as the declamatory opinions of recluse and splenetic men who had never tasted them at all, and consequently were thought no judges in the matter. So that 'tis no great wonder, if the greatest part of such reflections, however just in themselves and founded on truth and a knowledge of the world, are found to leave little impression where the imagination was already heated with great expectations of future happiness; and that the best lectures that have been read upon the vanity of the world, so seldom stop a man in pursuit of the object of his desire, or give him half the conviction, that the possession of it will, and what the experience of his own life, or a careful observation upon the life of others, do at length generally confirm to us all.

Let us endeavour then to try the cause upon this issue; and instead of recurring to the common arguments or taking any one's word in the case, let us trust to matter of fact; and if upon enquiry, it appears that the actions of mankind are not to be accounted for upon any other principle, but this of the insufficiency of our enjoyments, 'twill go further towards the establishment of the truth of this part of the discourse, than a thousand speculative arguments which might be offered on the occasion.

Now if we take a survey of the life of a man from the time he is come to reason, to the latest decline of it in old age—we shall find him engaged, and generally hurried on in such a succession of different pursuits, and different opinions of things, through the different stages of his life—as will admit of no explication, but this, that he finds no rest for the sole of his foot, on any of the plans where he has been led to expect it.

The moment he is got loose from tutors and governors, and is left to judge for himself, and pursue this scheme his own way— his first thoughts are generally full of the mighty happiness which he is going to enter upon, from the free enjoyment of the pleasures in which he sees others of his age and fortune engaged.

In consequence of this—take notice, how his imagination is caught by every glittering appearance that flatters this expectation. —Observe what impressions are made upon his senses, by diversions, music, dress, and beauty—and how his spirits are upon the wing, flying in pursuit of them; that you would think he could never have enough.

Leave him to himself a few years, till the edge of the appetite is worn down—and you will scarce know him again. You will find him entered into engagements, and setting up for a man of business and conduct, talking of no other happiness but what centres in projects of making the most of this world, and providing for his children, and children's children after them. Examine his notions, he will tell you, that the gayer pleasures of youth, are fit only for those who know not how to dispose of themselves and time to better advantage. That however fair and promising they might appear to a man unpractised in them—they were no better than a life of folly and impertinence, and so far from answering your expectations of happiness, 'twas well if you escaped without pain.—That in every experiment he had tried, he had found more bitter than sweet, and for the little pleasure one could snatch—it too often left a terrible sting behind it: Besides, did the ballance lay on the other side, he would tell you, there could be no true satisfaction where a life runs on in so giddy a circle, out of which a wise man should extricate himself as soon as he can, that he may begin to look forwards.— That it becomes a man of character and consequence to lay aside childish things, to take care of his interests, to establish the fortune of his family, and place it out of want and dependence: and in a word, if there is such a thing as happiness upon earth, it must consist in the accomplishment of this;—and for his own part, if GOD should prosper his endeavours so as to be worth such a sum, or to be able to bring such a point to bear—he shall be one of the happiest of the sons of men.—In full assurance of this, on he drudges—plots —contrives—rises early—late takes rest, and eats the bread of carefulness, till at length, by hard labour and perseverance, he has reached, if not outgone the object he had first in view.—When he has got thus far—if he is a plain and sincere man, he will make no scruple to acknowledge truly, what alteration he has found in himself—if you ask him—he will tell you, that his imagination painted something before his eyes, the reality of which he has not yet attained to: that with all the accumulations of his wealth, he neither lives the merrier, sleeps the sounder, or has less care and anxiety upon his spirits, than at his first setting out.

Perhaps, you'll say, some dignity, honour, or title only is wanting—Oh! could I accomplish that, as there would be nothing left then for me to wish, good GOD! how happy should I be! 'tis still the same—the dignity or title—though they crown his head with honor—add not one cubit to his happiness.—Upon summing up the account, all is found to be seated merely in the imagination.— The faster he has pursued, the faster the phantom fled before him, —and to use the Satyrist's comparison of the chariot wheels,— haste as they will, they must for ever keep the same distance.

But what? though I have been thus far disappointed in my expectations of happiness from the possession of riches—'Let me try, whether I shall not meet with it, in the spending and fashionable enjoyment of them.'

Behold! I will get me down, and make me great works, and build me houses, and plant me vineyards, and make me gardens and pools of water. And I will get me servants and maidens, and whatsoever my eyes desire, I will not keep from them.

In the prosecution of this—he drops all gainful pursuits—withdraws himself from the busy part of the world—realizes—pulls down—builds up again. Buys statues, pictures—plants—and plucks up by the roots—levels mountains—and fills up vallies—turns rivers into dry ground, and dry ground into rivers.—Says unto this man, go, and he goeth, and unto another, do this, and he doeth it,— and whatsoever his soul lusteth after of this kind, he witholds not from it. When every thing is thus planned by himself, and executed according to his wish and direction, surely he is arrived to the accomplishment of his wishes, and has got to the summit of all human happiness?—Let the most fortunate adventurers in this way, answer the question for him, and say—how often it rises higher than a bare and simple amusement—and well, if you can compound for that—since 'tis often purchased at so high a price, and so soured by a mixture of other incidental vexations, as to become too often a work of repentance, which in the end will extort the same sorrowful confession from him, which it did from Solomon, in the like case,—

Lo! I looked on all the works that my hands had wrought, and on the labour that I had laboured to do—and behold all was vanity and vexation of spirit—and there was no profit to me under the sun.[1]

To inflame this account the more—'twill be no miracle, if upon casting it up, he has gone further lengths than he first intended, run into expenses which have entangled his fortune, and brought himself into such difficulties as to make way for the last experiment he can try—and that is to turn miser, with no happiness in view but what is to rise out of the little designs of a sordid mind, set upon saving and scraping up all he has injudiciously spent.

In this last stage—behold him a poor trembling wretch, shut up from all mankind—sinking into utter contempt; spending careful days and sleepless nights in pursuit of what a narrow and contracted heart can never enjoy:—And let us here leave him to the conviction he will one day find—That there is no end of his labour—That his eyes will never be satisfied with riches, or will say—For whom do I labour and bereave myself of rest?—This is also a sore travel.

I believe this is no uncommon picture of the disappointments of human life—and the manner our pleasures and enjoyments slip from under us in every stage of our life. And though I would not be thought by it, as if I was denying the reality of pleasures, or disputing the being of them, any more, than one would, the reality of pain—Yet I must observe on this head, that there is a plain distinction to be made betwixt pleasure and happiness. For tho' there can be no happiness without pleasure—yet the reverse of the proposition will not hold true.—We are so made, that from the common gratifications of our appetites, and the impressions of a thousand objects, we snatch the one, like a transient gleam, without being suffered to taste the other, and enjoy the perpetual sun-shine and fair weather which constantly attend it. This, I contend, is only to be found in religion—in the consciousness of virtue—and the sure and certain hopes of a better life, which brightens all our prospects, and leaves no room to dread disappointments—because the expectation of it is built upon a rock, whose foundations are as deep as those of heaven and hell.

[1] close paraphrase from *Ecclesiastes* II, 11.

And tho' in our pilgrimage through this world—some of us may be so fortunate as to meet with some clear fountains by the way, that may cool for a few moments, the heat of this great thirst of happiness—yet our Saviour, who knew the world, tho' he enjoyed but little of it, tells us, that whosoever drinketh of this water will thirst again:—and we all find by experience it is so, and by reason that it always must be so.

I conclude this short observation upon Solomon's evidence in this case.

Never did the busy brain of a lean and hectic chymist search for the philosopher's stone with more pains and ardour than this great man did after happiness. He was one of the wisest enquirers into nature—had tried all her powers and capacities, and after a thousand vain speculations and vile experiments, he affirmed at length, it lay hid in no one thing he had tried—like the chymist's projections, all had ended in smoak, or what was worse, in vanity and vexation of spirit:—the conclusion of the whole matter was this— that he advises every man who would be happy, to fear God and keep his commandments.[1]

[1] *Ecclesiastes* XII, 13.

Sermon XVIII
THE LEVITE AND HIS CONCUBINE[1]

Judges XIX. 1, 2, 3.

And it came to pass in those days, when there was no king in Israel, that there was a certain Levite sojourning on the side of Mount Ephraim, who took unto him a concubine.

—A CONCUBINE!—but the text accounts for it, *for in those days there was no king in Israel,* and the Levite, you will say, like every other man in it, did what was right in his own eyes,—and so, you may add, did his concubine too,—*for she played the whore against him and went away.*—

—Then shame and grief go with her, and wherever she seeks a shelter, may the hand of justice shut the door against her.—

Not so; for she went unto her father's house in Bethlehem-judah, and was with him four whole months.—Blessed interval for meditation upon the fickleness and vanity of this world and its pleasures! I see the holy man upon his knees,—with hands compressed to his bosom, and with uplifted eyes, thanking heaven, that the object which had so long shared his affections, was fled.—

The text gives a different picture of his situation; *for he arose and went after her to speak friendly to her, and to bring her back again, having his servant with him, and a couple of asses; and she brought him unto her father's house; and when the father of the damsel saw him, he rejoiced to meet him.*—

—A most sentimental group! you'll say: and so it is, my good

---

[1] Sermon III in Volume II.

commentator, the world talks of every thing : give but the outlines of a story,—let *Spleen* or *Prudery* snatch the pencil, and they will finish it with so many hard strokes, and with so dirty a colouring, that *Candor* and *Courtesy* will sit in torture as they look at it.— Gentle and virtuous spirits! ye who know not what it is to be rigid interpreters, but of your own failings,—to you I address myself, the unhired advocates for the conduct of the misguided,—whence is it, that the world is not more jealous of your office? How often must ye repeat it, 'That such a one's doing so or so'—is not suffici- ent evidence by itself to overthrow the accused? That our actions stand surrounded with a thousand circumstances which do not pre- sent themselves at first sight;—that the first springs and motives which impell'd the unfortunate, lie deeper still;—and, that of the millions which every hour are arraign'd, thousands of them may have err'd merely from the *head*, and been actually outwitted into evil; and even when from the heart,—that the difficulties and tempta- tions under which they acted,—the force of the passions,—the suitableness of the object, and the many struggles of virtue before she fell,—may be so many appeals from justice to the judgement seat of pity.

Here then let us stop a moment, and give the story of the Levite and his Concubine a second hearing: like all others much of it de- pends upon the telling; and as the Scripture has left us no kind of comment upon it, 'tis a story on which the heart cannot be at a loss for what to say, or the imagination for what to suppose—the danger is, humanity may say too much.

And it came to pass in those days when there was no king in Israel, that a certain Levite sojourning on the side of Mount Ephraim, took unto himself a Concubine.—

O Abraham, thou father of the faithful! if this was wrong,— Why didst thou set so ensnaring an example before the eyes of thy descendants? and, Why did the GOD of Abraham, the GOD of Isaac and Jacob, bless so often the seed of such intercourses, and promise to multiply and make princes out of them?

GOD can dispense with his own laws; and accordingly we find the holiest of the patriarchs, and others in the Scripture whose hearts cleaved most unto GOD, accommodating themselves as well as they could to the dispensation: that Abraham had Hagar;—

that Jacob, besides his two wives, Rachel and Leah, took also unto him Zilpah and Bilhah, from whom many of the tribes descended:— that David had seven wives and ten concubines;—Rehoboam, sixty, —and that, in whatever cases it became reproachable, it seemed not so much the thing itself, as the abuse of it, which made it so; this was remarkable in that of Solomon, whose excess became an insult upon the privileges of mankind; for by the same plan of luxury, which made it necessary to have forty thousand stalls of horses,— he had unfortunately miscalculated his other wants, and so had seven hundred wives, and three hundred concubines.—

Wise—deluded man! was it not that thou madest some amends for thy bad practice, by thy good preaching, what had become of thee!—three hundred—but let us turn aside, I beseech you, from so sad a stumbling block.

The Levite had but one. The Hebrew word imports a woman a concubine, or a wife a concubine, to distinguish her from the more infamous species, who came under the roofs of the licentious without principle. Our annotators tell us, that in Jewish *œconomicks*, these differ'd little from the wife, except in some outward ceremonies and stipulations, but agreed with her in all the true essences of marriage, and gave themselves up to the husband (for so he is call'd) with faith plighted, with sentiments and with affection.

Such a one the Levite wanted to share his solitude, and fill up that uncomfortable blank in the heart in such a situation; for not-withstanding all we meet with in books, in many of which, no doubt, there are a good many handsome things said upon the sweets of retirement, &c . . . yet still, *'it is not good for man to be alone':*[1] nor can all which the cold-hearted pedant stuns our ears with upon the subject, ever give one answer of satisfaction to the mind; in the midst of the loudest vauntings of philosophy, Nature will have her yearnings for society and friendship;—a good heart wants some object to be kind to—and the best parts of our blood, and the purest of our spirits suffer most under destitution.

Let the torpid Monk seek heaven comfortless and alone.—GOD speed him! For my own part, I fear, I should never so find the way: let me be wise and religious—but let me be MAN: wherever thy

[1] *Genesis* II, 18.

Providence places me, or whatever be the road I take to get to thee —give me some companion in my journey, be it only to remark to, How our shadows lengthen as the sun goes down;—to whom I may say, How fresh is the face of nature! How sweet the flowers of the field! How delicious are these fruits!

Alas! with bitter herbs, like his passover,[1] did the Levite eat them: for as they thus walked the path of life together,—she wantonly turn'd aside unto another, and fled from him.

It is the mild and quiet half of the world, who are generally outraged and borne down by the other half of it: but in this they have the advantage; whatever be the sense of their wrongs, that pride stands not so watchful a sentinel over their forgiveness, as it does in the breasts of the fierce and froward: we should all of us, I believe, be more forgiving than we are, would the world but give us leave; but it is apt to interpose in its ill offices in remissions, especially of this kind: the truth is, it has its laws, to which the heart is not always a party; and acts so like an unfeeling engine in all cases without distinction, that it requires all the firmness of the most settled humanity to bear up against it.

Many a bitter conflict would the Levite have to sustain with himself—his Concubine—and the sentiments of his tribe, upon the wrong done him:—much matter for pleading—and many an embarrassing account on all sides: in a period of four whole months, every passion would take its empire by turns; and in the ebbs and flows of the less unfriendly ones, PITY would find some moments to be heard—RELIGION herself would not be silent,—CHARITY would have much to say,—and thus attun'd, every object he beheld on the borders of mount Ephraim,—every grot and grove he pass'd by, would solicit the recollection of former kindness, and awaken an advocate in her behalf, more powerful than them all.

'I grant—I grant it all'—he would cry,—''tis foul! 'tis faithless!'—but, Why is the door of mercy to be shut forever against it? and, Why is it to be the only sad crime that the injured may not remit, or reason or imagination pass over without a scar?—Is it the blackest? In what catalogue of human offenses is it so marked? or, Is it, that of all others, 'tis a blow most grievous to be endured?—

[1] At the seder meal of Passover, Jews taste of the bitter herbs to recall the afflictions of the slaves in Egypt.

the heart cries out, It is so: but let me ask my own, What passions are they which give edge and force to this weapon which has struck me? and, Whether it is not my own pride, as much as my virtues, which at this moment excite the greatest part of that intolerable anguish in the wound which I am laying to her charge? But merciful heaven! was it otherwise, Why is an unhappy creature of thine to be persecuted by me with so much cruel revenge and rancorous despite as my first transport called for? Have faults no extenuations? —Makes it nothing, that, when the trespass was committed, she forsook the partner of her guilt, and fled directly to her father's house? And is there no difference betwixt one propensely going out of the road and continuing there, through depravity of will—and a hapless wanderer straying by delusion, and warily treading back her steps?—Sweet is the look of sorrow for an offence, in a heart determined never to commit it more!—Upon that altar only, could I offer up my wrongs. Cruel is the punishment which an ingenuous mind will take upon itself, from the remorse of so hard a trespass against me,—and if that will not balance the account,—just GOD! let me forgive the rest. Mercy well becomes the heart of all thy creatures,—but most of thy servant, a Levite, who offers up so many daily sacrifices to thee, for the transgressions of thy people.—

—'But to little purpose,' he would add, 'have I served at thy altar, where my business was to sue for mercy, had I not learn'd to practise it.'

Peace and happiness rest upon the head and heart of every man who can thus think!

So he arose, and went after her to speak friendly to her—in the original—'to speak to her heart';—to apply to their former endearments,—and to ask, How she could be so unkind to him, and so very unkind to herself?—

—Even the upbraidings of the quiet and relenting are sweet: not like the strivings of the fierce and inexorable, who bite and devour all who have thwarted them in their way;—but they are calm and courteous like the spirit which watches over their character: How can such a temper woo the damsel and not bring her back? or, How could the father of the damsel, in such a scene, have a heart open to any impressions but those mentioned in the text;—*That when he saw him, he rejoiced to meet him*;—urged his stay from day to day, with the most irresistible of all invitations,—*'Comfort thy heart, and tarry all night, and let thine heart be merry.'*

If *Mercy* and *Truth* thus met together in settling this account, *Love* would surely be of the party: great—great is its power in cementing what has been broken, and wiping out wrongs even from the memory itself: and so it was—for the Levite arose up, and with him his Concubine and his servant, and they departed.

It serves no purpose to pursue the story further; the catastrophe is horrid; and would lead us beyond the particular purpose for which I have enlarged upon thus much of it,—and that is, to discredit rash judgement, and illustrate from the manner of conducting this drama, the courtesy which the *dramatis personæ* of every other piece, may have a right to. Almost one half of our time is spent in telling and hearing evil of one another—some unfortunate knight is always upon the stage—and every hour brings forth something strange and terrible to fill up our discourse and our astonishment, 'How people can be so foolish!'—and 'tis well if the compliment ends there: so that there is not a social virtue for which there is so constant a demand,—or, consequently, so well worth cultivating, as that which opposes this unfriendly current—many and rapid are the springs which feed it, and various and sudden, GOD knows, are the guests which render it unsafe to us in this short passage of our life: let us make the discourse as servicable as we can, by tracing some of the most remarkable of them, up to their source.

And first, there is one miserable inlet to this evil, and which by the way, if speculation is supposed to precede practice, may have been derived, for aught I know, from some of our busiest enquirers after nature,—and that is, when with more zeal than knowledge, we account for the phenomena, before we are sure of their existence. —*It is not the manner of the Romans to condemn any man to death* (much less to be martyr'd), said Festus;—*and doth our law judge any man before it hear him, and know what he doth*? cried Nicodemus; *and he that answereth, or determineth, a matter before he has heard it,— it is folly and a shame unto him.*—We are generally in such a haste to make our own decrees, that we pass over the justice of these,— and then the scene is so changed by it, that 'tis our folly only which is real, and that of the accused, which is imaginary: through too much precipitancy it will happen so;—and then the jest is spoiled

—or we have criticised our own shadow.

A second way is, when the process goes on more orderly, and we begin with getting information,—but do it from those suspected evidences, against which our SAVIOUR warns us, when he bids us *'not to judge according to appearance:'*—in truth, 'tis behind these, that most of the things which blind human judgement lie concealed, —and on the contrary, there are many things which appear to be,— which are not:—*Christ came eating and drinking,—behold a wine-bibber!*—he sat with sinners—he was their friend:—in many cases of which kind, *Truth*, like a modest matron, scorns art—and disdains to press herself forwards into the circle to be seen:—ground sufficient for *Suspicion* to draw up the libel,—for *Malice* to give the torture,—or rash *Judgement* to start up and pass a final sentence.

A third way is, when the facts which denote misconduct, are less disputable, but are commented upon with an asperity of censure, which a humane or a gracious temper would spare: an abhorrence against what is criminal, is so fair a plea for this, and looks so like virtue in the face, that in a sermon against rash judgement, it would be unseasonable to call it in question,—and yet, I declare, in the fullest torrent of exclamations which the guilty can deserve, that the simple ápostrophè, 'Who made me to differ: why was not I an example?' would touch my heart more, and give me a better earnest of the commentators,—than the most corrosive period you could add. The punishment of the unhappy, I fear, is enough without it— and were it not,—'tis piteous, the tongue of a Christian, whose religion is all candour and courtesy, should be made the executioner. We find in the discourse between Abraham and the rich man, tho' one was in heaven, and the other in hell, yet still the patriarch treated him with mild language:—*Son!—Son, remember that thou in thy lifetime, &c. &c.*[1]—and in a dispute about the body of Moses, between the Arch-angel and the devil, (himself,) St. Jude tells us, he durst not bring a railing accusation against him;—'twas unworthy of his high character,[2]—and indeed, might have been impolitick too; for if he had (as one of our divines notes upon the passage) the devil had been too hard for him at railing,—'twas his

[1] *Luke*, XVI, 25.
[2] *Jude*, 9.

own weapon,—and the basest spirits after his example are the most expert at it.

This leads me to the observation of a fourth cruel inlet to this evil, and that is, the desire of being thought men of wit and parts, and the vain expectation of coming honestly by the title, by shrewd and sarcastick reflections upon whatever is done in the world. This is setting up trade upon the broken stock of other people's failings, —perhaps their misfortunes:—so much good may't do them with what honor they can get,—the furthest extent of which, I think, is, to be praised, as we do some sauces, with tears in our eyes: It is a commerce most illiberal; and as it requires no vast capital, too many embark in it, and so long as there are bad passions to be gratified,— and bad heads to judge, with such it may pass for wit, or at least like some vile relation, whom all the family is ashamed of, claim kindred with it, even in better companies. Whatever be the degree of its affinity, it has helped to give wit a bad name, as if the main essence of it was satire: certainly there is a difference between *Bitterness* and *Saltness*,—that is,—between malignity and the festivity of wit,—the one is a mere quickness of apprehension, void of humanity,—and is a talent of the devil; the other comes down from the Father of Spirits, so pure and abstracted from persons, that willingly hurts no man; or if it touches upon indecorum, 'tis with that dexterity of true genius, which enables him rather to give a new colour to the absurdity, and let it pass.—He may smile at the shape of the obelisk raised to another's fame,—but the malignant wit will level it at once with the ground, and build his own upon the ruins of it.—

What then, ye rash censurers of the world! Have ye no mansions for your credit, but those from whence ye have extruded the right owners? Are there no regions for you to shine in, that ye descend for it into the low caverns of abuse and crimination? Have ye no seats—but those of the scornful to sit down in? If *Honour* has mistook his road, or the *Virtues*, in their excesses, have approached too near the confines of VICE, Are they therefore to be cast down the precipice? Must BEAUTY for ever be trampled upon in the dirt for one—one false step? And shall no one virtue or good quality, out of the thousand the fair penitent may have left,—shall not one of them be suffered to stand by her?—Just GOD of Heaven and Earth!——

    —But thou art merciful, loving and righteous, and lookest down with pity upon these wrongs thy servants do unto each other: pardon us, we beseech thee, for them, and all our transgressions; let it not be remember'd, that we were brethren of the same flesh, the same feelings and infirmities.—O my GOD! write it not down in thy book, that thou madest us merciful after thy own image;—that thou hast given us a religion so courteous,—so good temper'd,—that every precept of it carries a balm along with it to heal the soreness of our natures, and sweeten our spirits, that we might live with such kind intercourse in this world, as will fit us to exist together in a better.

Sermon II
THE HOUSE OF FEASTING AND THE HOUSE OF MOURNING DESCRIBED[1]

Ecclesiastes VII. 2, 3.
It is better to go to the house of mourning, than to the house of feasting.—

THAT I deny—but let us hear the wise man's reasoning upon it—
for that is *the end of all men, and the living* will *lay it to* his *heart:
sorrow is better than laughter*—for a crack'd brain'd order of Carthu-
sian monks, I grant, but not for men of the world: For what purpose
do you imagine, has GOD made us? for the social sweets of the well
watered vallies, where he has planted us, or for the dry and dismal
deserts of the *Sierra Morena*? are the sad accidents of life, and the
uncheery hours which perpetually overtake us, are they not enough,
but we must sally forth in quest of them,—belie our own hearts,
and say, as your text would have us, that they are better than those
of joy? did the Best of Beings send us into the world for this end—
to go weeping through it,—to vex and shorten a life short and
vexatious enough already? do you think my good preacher, that he
who is infinitely happy, can envy us our enjoyments? or that a
Being so infinitely kind would grudge a mournful traveller, the
short rest and refreshments necessary to support his spirits through
the stages of a weary pilgrimage? or that he would call him to a
severe reckoning, because in his way he had hastily snatch'd at some
little fugacious pleasures, merely to sweeten this uneasy journey of
life, and reconcile him to the ruggedness of the road, and the many

[1] Highly derivative from Sterne's 'Penances', which appeared posthumously as Sermon 10 in Volume VI.

hard justlings he is sure to meet with? Consider, I beseech you, what provision and accomodation, the Author of our being has prepared for us, that we might not go on our way sorrowing—how many caravanserai of rest—what powers and faculties he has given us for taking it—what apt objects he has placed in our way to entertain us;—some of which he has made so fair, so exquisitely for this end, that they have power over us for a time to charm away the sense of pain, to cheer up the dejected heart under poverty and sickness, and make it go and remember its miseries no more.

I will not contend at present against this rhetorick; I would choose rather for a moment to go on with the allegory, and say we are travellers, and, in the most affecting sense of that idea, that like travellers, though upon business of the last and nearest concern to us, may surely be allowed to amuse ourselves with the natural or artificial beauties of the country we are passing through, without reproach of forgetting the main errand we are sent upon; and if we can so order it, as not to be led out of the way, by the variety of prospects, edifices, and ruins which solicit us, it would be a nonsensical piece of saint errantry to shut our eyes.

But let us not lose sight of the argument in pursuit of the simile.

Let us remember various as our excursions are,—that we still set our faces towards Jerusalem—that we have a place of rest and happiness, towards which we hasten, and that the way to get there is not so much to please our hearts, as to improve them in virtue;—that mirth and feasting are usually no friends to achievements of this kind—but that a season of affliction is in some sort a season of piety—not only because our sufferings are apt to put us in mind of our sins, but that by the check and interruption which they give our pursuits, they allow us what the hurry and bustle of the world too often deny us,—and that is a little time for reflection, which is all that most of us want to make us wiser and better men;—that at certain times it is so necessary a man's mind should be turned towards itself, that rather than want occasions, he had better purchase them at the expence of his present happiness.—He had better, as the text expresses it, *go to the house of mourning*, where he will meet with something to subdue his passions, than to the house of feasting, where the joy and gaiety of the place is likely to excite them.— That whereas the entertainments and caresses of the one place, expose his heart and lay it open to temptations—the sorrows of the other defend it, and as naturally shut them from it. So strange and unaccountable a creature is man! he is so framed, that he cannot but pursue happiness—and yet unless he is made sometimes miserable, how apt is he to mistake the way which can only lead him to the accomplishment of his own wishes!

This is the full force of the wise man's declaration.—But to do farther justice to his words, I would endeavour to bring the subject still nearer.—For which purpose, it will be necessary to stop here, and take a transient view of the two places here referred to,—the house of mourning, and the house of feasting. Give me leave therefore, I beseech you, to recall both of them for a moment, to your imaginations, that from thence I may appeal to your hearts, how faithfully, and upon what good grounds, the effects and natural operations of each upon our minds are intimated in the text.

And first, let us look into the house of feasting.

And here, to be as fair and candid as possible in the description of this, we will not take it from the worst originals, such as are opened merely for the sale of virtue, and so calculated for the end, that the disguise each is under not only gives power safely to drive on the bargain, but safely carry it into execution too.

This, we will not suppose to be the case—nor let us even imagine, the house of feasting to be such a scene of intemperance and excess, as the house of feasting does often exhibit;—but let us take it from one, as little exceptionable as we can—where there is, or at least appears nothing really criminal,—but where every thing seems to be kept within the visible bounds of moderation and sobriety.

Imagine then, such a house of feasting, where either by consent or invitation a number of each sex is drawn together for no other purpose but the enjoyment and mutual entertainment of each other, which we will suppose shall arise from no other pleasures but what custom authorises, and religion does not absolutely forbid.

Before we enter—let us examine, what must be the sentiments of each individual previous to his arrival, and we shall find that however they may differ from one another in tempers and opinions, that every one seems to agree in this—that he is going to a house dedicated to joy and mirth, it was fit he should divest himself of whatever was likely to contradict that intention, or be inconsistent with it.—That for this purpose, he had left his cares—his serious thoughts—and his moral reflections behind him, and was come forth from home with only such dispositions and gaiety of heart as suited the occasion, and promoted the intended mirth and jollity of the place. With this preparation of mind, which is as little as can be supposed, since it will amount to no more than a desire in each to render himself an acceptable guest,—let us conceive them entering into the house of feasting, with hearts set loose from grave restraints, and open to the expectations of receiving pleasure. It is not necessary, as I premised, to bring intemperance into this scene— or to suppose such an excess in the gratification of the appetites as shall ferment the blood and set the desires in a flame:—Let us admit no more of it therefore, than will gently stir them, and fit them for the impressions which so benevolent a commerce will naturally excite. In this disposition thus wrought upon beforehand and already improved to this purpose,—take notice, how mechanically the thoughts and spirits rise—how soon, and insensibly, they are got above the pitch and first bounds which cooler hours would have marked.

When the gay and smiling aspect of things has begun to leave the passages to a man's heart thus thoughtlessly unguarded—when kind and caressing looks of every object without that can flatter his senses, have conspired with the enemy within to betray him, and put him off his defence—when music likewise hath lent her aid, and tried her power upon his passions—when the voice of singing men, and the voice of singing women with the sound of the viol and the lute have broken in upon his soul, and in some tender notes have touched the secret springs of rapture—that moment let us direct and look into his heart—see how vain! how weak! how empty a thing it is! Look through its several recesses,—those pure mansions formed for the reception of innocence and virtue—sad spectacle! Behold those fair inhabitants now dispossessed—turned out of their sacred dwellings to make room—for what?—at the best for levity and indiscretion—perhaps for folly—it may be for more impure guests, which possibly in so general a riot of the mind and senses may take occasion to enter unsuspected at the same time.

In a scene and disposition thus described—can the most cautious say—thus far shall my desires go—and no farther? or will the coolest and most circumspect say, when pleasure has taken full possession of his heart, that no thought nor purpose shall arise there, which he would have concealed?—In those loose and unguarded moments the imagination is not always at command—in spite of reason and reflection, it will forceably carry him sometimes whither he would not—like the unclean spirit, in the parent's sad description of his child's case, which took him, and oft times cast him into the fire to destroy him, and wheresoever it taketh him, it teareth him, and hardly departeth from him.[1]

But this, you'll say, is the worst account of what the mind may suffer here.

Why may we not make more favorable suppositions?—that numbers by exercise and custom to such encounters, learn gradually to despise and triumph over them;—that the minds of many are not so susceptible of warm impressions, or so badly fortified against them, that pleasure should easily corrupt or soften them;—that it would be hard to suppose, of the great multitudes which daily throng and press into this house of feasting, but that numbers come out of it again, with *all* the innocence with which they entered;— and that if both sexes are included in the computation, what *fair* examples shall we see of many of so pure and chaste a turn of mind— that the house of feasting, with all its charms and temptations, was never able to excite a thought, or awaken an inclination which virtue need blush at—or which the most scrupulous conscience might not support. God forbid we should say otherwise:—no doubt, numbers of all ages escape unhurt, and get off this dangerous sea without shipwreck. Yet, are they not to be reckoned amongst the more fortunate adventurers?—and though one would not absolutely prohibit the attempt, or be so cynical as to condemn every one who tries it, since there are so many I suppose who cannot well do otherwise, and whose condition and situation in life unavoidably force them upon it—yet we may be allowed to describe this fair and flattering coast—we may point out the unsuspected dangers of it, and warn the unwary passenger, where they lay. We may shew him what hazards his youth and inexperience will run, how little he can gain by the venture, and how much wiser and better it would

[1] *Mark* IX, 17, 18.

be [as is implied in the text] to seek occasions rather to improve his little stock of virtue than incautiously expose it to so unequal a chance, where the best he can hope is to return safe with what treasure he carried out—but where probably, he may be so unfortunate as to lose it all—be lost himself, and undone for ever.

Thus much for the house of feasting; which, by the way, though generally open at other times of the year throughout the world, is supposed in christian countries, now every where to be universally shut up. And, in truth, I have been more full in my cautions against it, not only as reason requires,—but in reverence to this season* wherein our church exacts a more particular forbearance and self-denial in this point, and thereby adds to the restraints upon pleasure and entertainments which this representation of things has suggested against them already.

Here then, let us turn aside, from this gay scene; and suffer me to take you with me for a moment to one much fitter for your meditation. Let us go into the house of mourning, made so, by such afflictions as have been brought in, merely by the common cross accidents and disasters to which our condition is exposed,—where perhaps, the aged parents sit broken hearted, pierced to their souls with the folly and indiscretion of a thankless child—the child of their prayers, in whom all their hopes and expectations centred:—perhaps a more affecting scene—a virtuous family lying pinched with want, where the unfortunate support of it, having long struggled with a train of misfortunes, and bravely fought up against them—is now piteously borne down at the last—overwhelmed with a cruel blow which no forecast or frugality could have prevented.—O GOD! look upon his afflictions.—Behold him distracted with many sorrows, surrounded with the tender pledges of his love, and the partner of his cares—without bread to give them,—unable, from the remembrance of better days, to dig;—to beg, ashamed.

When we enter into the house of mourning such as this,—it is impossible to insult the unfortunate even with an improper look—under whatever levity and dissipation of heart. Such objects catch our eyes,—they catch likewise our attentions, collect and call home our scattered thoughts, and exercise them with wisdom. A transient

* Preached in *Lent*.

scene of distress, such as is here sketch'd, how soon does it furnish materials to set the mind at work? how necessarily does it engage it to the consideration of the miseries and misfortunes, the dangers and calamities to which the life of man is subject? By holding up such a glass before it, it forces the mind to see and reflect upon the vanity, —the perishing condition and uncertain tenure of every thing in this world. From reflections of this serious cast, the thoughts insensibly carry us farther—and from considering, what we are—what kind of world we live in, and what evils befall us in it, they set us to look forwards at what possibly we shall be—for what kind of world we are intended—what evils may befall us there—and what provision we should make against them, here, whilst we have time and opportunity.

If these lessons are so inseparable from the house of mourning here supposed—we shall find it a still more instructive school of wisdom when we take a view of the place in that more affecting light in which the wise man seems to confine it in the text, in which, by the house of mourning, I believe, he means that particular scene of sorrow where there is lamentation and mourning for the dead.

Turn in hither, I beseech you, for a moment. Behold a dead man ready to be carried out, the only son of his mother, and she a widow. Perhaps a more affecting spectacle—a kind and indulgent father of a numerous family, lies breathless—snatched away in the strength of his age—torn in an evil hour from his children and the bosom of a disconsolate wife.

Behold much people of the city gathered together to mix their tears, with settled sorrow in their looks, going heavily along to the house of mourning, to perform that last melancholy office, which when the debt of nature is payed, we are called upon to pay each other.

If this sad occasion which leads him there, has not done it already, take notice, to what a serious and devout frame of mind every man is reduced, the moment he enters this gate of affliciton. The busy and fluttering spirits, which in the house of mirth were wont to transport him from one diverting object to another—see how they are fallen! how peaceably they are laid! In this gloomy mansion full of shades and uncomfortable damps to seize the soul—see, the light and easy heart, which never knew what it was to think before, how pensive it is now, how soft, how susceptible, how full of religious impressions, how deeply it is smitten with sense and with a love of virtue. Could we, in this crisis, whilst this empire of reason and religion lasts, and the heart is thus excited with wisdom and busied with heavenly contemplations—could we see it naked as it is—stripped of all its passions, unspotted by the world, and regardless of its pleasures—we might then safely rest our cause, upon this single evidence, and appeal to the most sensual, whether Solomon has not made a just determination here, in favour of the house of mourning?—not for its own sake, but as it is fruitful in virtue, and becomes the occasion of so much good. Without this end, sorrow I own has no use, but to shorten a man's days—nor can gravity, with all its studied solemnity of look and carriage, serve any end but to make one half of the world merry, and impose upon the other.

Consider what has been said, and may GOD of his mercy bless you. Amen.

Sermon III
PHILANTHROPY RECOMMENDED

Luke X. 36, 37.
Which now of these three, thinkest thou, was neighbor unto him that fell amongst thieves?—And he said, he that shewed mercy on him. Then said Jesus unto him—Go, and do thou likewise.

IN THE foregoing verses of this chapter, the Evangelist relates, that a certain lawyer stood up and tempted JESUS, saying, master, what shall I do to inherit eternal life?—To which enquiry, our SAVIOUR, as his manner was, when any ensnaring question was put to him, which he saw proceeded more from a design to entangle him, than an honest view of getting information—instead of giving a direct answer which might afford a handle to malice, or at best serve only to gratify an impertinent humour—he immediately retorts the question upon the man who asked it, and unavoidably puts him upon the necessity of answering himself;—and as in the present case, the particular profession of the enquirer, and his supposed general knowledge of all other branches of learning, left no room to suspect, he could be ignorant of the true answer to this question, and especially of what every one knew was delivered upon that head by their great Legislator, our SAVIOUR therefore refers him to his own memory of what he had found there in the course of his studies.—What is written in the law, how readest thou?— upon which the enquirer reciting the general heads of our duty to GOD and MAN as delivered in the 18th of Leviticus and the 6th of Deuteronomy,—namely,—*That we should worship the Lord our God with all our hearts, and love our neighbor as ourselves*; our blessed

Saviour tells him, he had answered right, and if he followed that lesson, he could not fail of the blessing he seemed desirous to inherit. —*This do, and thou shalt live.*

But he, as the context tells us, willing to justify himself—willing possibly to gain more credit in the conference, or hoping perhaps to hear such a partial and narrow definition of the word *neighbor* as would suit his own principles, and justify some particular oppressions of his own, or those of which his whole order lay under an accusation—says unto Jesus in the 29th verse,—*And who is my neighbor?* though the demand at first may seem utterly trifling, yet it was far from being so in fact. For according as you understood the term in a more or less restrained sense—it produced many necessary variations in the duties you owed from that relation.—Our blessed Saviour, to rectify any partial and pernicious mistake in this matter, and place at once this duty of the love of our neighbor upon its true bottom of philanthropy and universal kindness, makes answer to the proposed question, not by any far-fetch'd refinement from the schools of the Rabbis, which might have sooner silenced than convinced the man—but by a direct appeal to human nature in an instance he relates of a man falling amongst thieves, left in the greatest distress imaginable, till by chance a Samaritan, an utter stranger, coming where he was, by an act of great goodness and compassion, not only relieved him at present, but took him under his protection, and generously provided for his future safety.

On the close of which engaging account—our Saviour appeals to the man's own heart in the first verse of the text—*Which now of these three thinkest thou was neighbor unto him that fell amongst thieves?* and instead of drawing the inference himself, leaves him to decide in favour of so noble a principle so evidently founded in mercy.—The lawyer, struck with the truth and justice of the doctrine, and frankly acknowledging the force of it, our blessed Saviour concludes the debate with a short admonition, that he would practise what he had approved—and go, and imitate that fair example of universal benevolence which it had set before him.

In the remaining part of the discourse I shall follow the same plan; and therefore shall beg leave to enlarge upon the story itself, with such reflections as will rise from it; and conclude, as our

Saviour has done, with the same exhortation to kindness and humanity which so naturally falls from it.

A certain man, says our Saviour, went down from Jerusalem to Jericho and fell among thieves, who stripped him of his rayment and departed, leaving him half dead. There is something in our nature which engages us to take part in every accident to which man is subject, from what cause soever it may have happened; but in such calamities as a man has fallen into through mere misfortune, to be charged upon no fault or indiscretion of himself, there is something then so truly interesting, that at the first sight we generally make them our own, not altogether from a reflection that they might have been or may be so, but oftener from a certain generosity and tenderness of nature which disposes us for compassion, abstracted from all considerations of self. So that without any observable act of will, we suffer with the unfortunate, and feel a weight upon our spirits we know not why, on seeing the most common instances of their distress. But where the spectacle is uncommonly tragical, and complicated with many circumstances of misery, the mind is then taken captive at once, and, *were* it inclined to it, has no power to make resistance, but surrenders itself to all the tender emotions of pity and deep concern. So that when one considers this friendly part of our nature without looking farther, one would think it impossible for a man to look upon misery, without finding himself in some measure attached to the interest of him who suffers it.—I say, one would think it impossible—for there are some tempers—how shall I describe them?—formed either of such impenetrable matter, or wrought up by habitual selfishness to such an utter insensibility of what becomes of the fortunes of their fellow-creatures, as if they were not partakers of the same nature, or had no lot or connection at all with the species.

Of this character, our Saviour produces two disgraceful instances in the behaviour of a priest and a Levite, whom in this account he represents as coming to the place where the unhappy man was— both passing by without either stretching forth a hand to assist, or uttering a word to comfort him in his distress.

And by chance there came down a certain priest!—merciful God! that a teacher of thy religion should ever want humanity— or that a man whose head might be thought full of the one, should have a heart void of the other!—This however was the case before us—and though in theory one would scarce suspect that the least pretence to religion and an open disregard to so main a part of it, could ever meet together in one person—yet in fact it is no fictitious character.

Look into the world—how often do you behold a sordid wretch, whose strait heart is open to no man's affliction, taking shelter behind an appearance of piety, and putting on the garb of religion, which none but the merciful and compassionate have a title to wear. Take notice with what sanctity he goes to the end of his days, in the same selfish track in which he first set out—turning neither to the right hand nor to the left—but plods on—pores all his life long upon the ground, as if afraid to look up, lest peradventure he should see aught which might turn him one moment out of that strait line where interest is carrying him—or if, by chance, he stumbles upon a hapless object of distress, which threatens such a disaster to him— like the man here presented, *devoutly* passing by on the other side, as if unwilling to trust himself to the impressions of nature, or hazard the inconveniences which pity might lead him into upon the occasion.

There is but one stroke wanting in this picture of an unmerciful man to render the character utterly odious, and that our SAVIOUR gives it in the following instance he relates upon it. And likewise, says he, *a Levite, when he was at the place, came and looked at him.* It was not a transient oversight, the hasty or ill-advised neglect of an unconsidering humour, with which the best disposed are sometimes overtaken, and led on beyond the point where otherwise they would have wished to stop.—NO!—on the contrary, it had all the aggravation of a deliberate act of insensibility proceeding from a hard heart. When he was at the place, he came, and looked at him —considered his misfortunes, gave time for reason and nature to have awoke—saw the imminent danger he was in—and the pressing necessity of immediate help, which so violent a case called aloud for —and after all—turned aside and unmercifully left him to all the distresses of his condition.

In all unmerciful actions, the worst of men pay this compliment at least to humanity, as to endeavour to wear as much of the appearance of it, as the case will well let them—so that in the hardest acts

a man shall be guilty of, he has some motives true or false always
ready to offer, either to satisfy himself or the world, and, GOD
knows, too often to impose both upon the one and the other. And
therefore it would be no hard matter here to give a probable guess
at what passed in the Levite's mind in the present case, and shew,
was it necessary, by what kind of casuistry he settled the matter
with his conscience as he passed by, and guarded all the passages to
his heart against the inroads which pity might attempt to make upon
the occasion.—But it is painful to dwell long upon this disagreeable
part of the story; I therefore hasten to the concluding incident of it,
which is so amiable that one cannot easily be too copious in reflections upon it.—And behold, says our SAVIOUR, a certain Samaritan
as he journeyed came where he was; and when he saw him he had
compassion on him—and went to him—bound up his wounds,
pouring in oil and wine—set him upon his own beast, brought him
to an inn and took care of him. I suppose, it will be scarce necessary
here to remind you that the Jews had no dealings with the Samari-
tans—an old religious grudge—the worst of all grudges, had
wrought such a dislike between both people, that they held themselves mutually discharged not only from all offices of friendship
and kindness, but even from the most common acts of courtesy
and good manners. This operated so strongly in our SAVIOUR's
time, that the woman of Samaria seemed astonished that he, being a
Jew, should *ask* water of her who was a Samaritan;[1] so that with
such a prepossession, however distressful the case of the unfortunate
man was, and how reasonably soever he might plead for pity from
another man, there was little aid or consolation to be looked for
from so unpromising a quarter. *Alas! after I have been twice passed
by, neglected by men of my own nation and religion bound by so many
ties to assist me, left here friendless and unpitied both by a Priest and a
Levite, men whose profession and superior advantages of knowledge
could not leave them in the dark in what manner they should discharge
this debt which my condition claims—after this—what hopes? what
expectations from a passenger, not only a stranger,—but a Samaritan
released from all obligations to me, and by a national dislike inflamed
by mutual ill offices, now made my enemy, and more likely to rejoice at*

[1] *John* IV, 7.

the evils which have fallen upon me, than to stretch forth a hand to save me from them.

'Tis no unnatural soliloquy to imagine; but the actions of generous and compassionate tempers baffle all little reasonings about them.—True charity, in the apostle's description, as it is kind, and is not easily provoked, so it manifested this character—for we find when he came where he was, and beheld his distress,—all the unfriendly passions, which at another time might have rose within him, now utterly forsook him and fled: when he saw his misfortunes—he forgot his enmity towards the man,—dropped all the prejudices which education had planted against him, and in the room of them, all that was good and compassionate was suffered to speak in his behalf.

In benevolent natures the impulse to pity is so sudden, that like instruments of music which only obey the touch—the objects which are fitted to excite such impressions work so instantaneous an effect, that you would think the will was scarce concerned, and that the mind was altogether passive in the sympathy which her own goodness has excited. The truth is,—the soul is generally in such cases so busily taken up and wholly engrossed by the object of pity, that she does not attend to her own operations, or take leisure to examine the principles upon which she acts. So that the Samaritan, though the moment he saw him he had compassion on him, yet sudden as the emotion is represented, you are not to imagine that it was mechanical, but that there was a settled principle of humanity and goodness which operated within him, and influenced not only the first impulse of kindness, but the continuation of it throughout the rest of so engaging a behaviour. And because it is a pleasure to look into a good mind, and trace out as far as one is able what passes within it on such occasions, I shall beg leave for a moment, to state an account of what was likely to pass in his, and in what manner so distressful a case would necessarily work upon such a disposition.

As he approached the place where the unfortunate man lay, the instant he beheld him, no doubt some such train of reflections as this would rise in his mind.

'Good God! what a spectacle of misery do I behold—a man stripped of his raiment—wounded—lying languishing before me upon the ground just ready to expire,—without the comfort of a friend to support him in his last agonies, or the prospect of a hand to close his eyes when his pains are over. But perhaps my concern should lessen when I reflect on the relations in which we stand to each other—that he is a Jew and I a Samaritan.—But are we not still both men? partakers of the same nature—and subject to the same evils?—let me change conditions with him for a moment and consider, had his lot befallen me as I journeyed in the way, what measure I should have expected at his hand.—Should I wish when he beheld me wounded and half-dead, that he should shut up his bowels of compassion from me, and double the weight of my miseries by passing by and leaving them unpitied?—But I am a stranger to the man—be it so—but I am no stranger to his condition—misfortunes are of no particular tribe or nation, but belong to us all, and have a general claim upon us, without distinction of climate, country or religion. Besides, though I am a stranger—'tis no fault of his that I do not know him, and therefore unequitable he should suffer by it:— Had I known him, possibly I should have had cause to love and pity him the more—for aught I know, he is some one of uncommon merit, whose life is rendered still more precious, as the lives and happiness of others may be involved in it: perhaps in this instant that he lies here forsaken, in all this misery, a whole virtuous family is joyfully looking for his return, and affectionately counting the hours of his delay. Oh! did they know what evil had befallen him—how would they fly to succour him.—Let me then hasten to supply those tender offices of binding up his wounds, and carrying him to a place of safety—or if that assistance comes too late, I shall comfort him at least in his last hour—and, if I can do nothing else, I shall soften his misfortunes by dropping a tear of pity over them.'

'Tis almost necessary to imagine the good Samaritan was influenced by some such thoughts as these, from the uncommon generosity of his behaviour, which is represented by our SAVIOUR operating like the warm zeal of a brother, mixed with the affectionate discretion and care of a parent, who was not satisfied with taking him under his protection, and supplying his present wants, but in looking forwards for him, and taking care that his wants should be supplied when he should be gone, and no longer near to befriend him.

I think there needs no stronger argument to prove how universally and deeply the seeds of this virtue of compassion are planted in the heart of man, than in the pleasure we take in such representations of it: and though some men have represented human nature in other colours, (though to what end I know not) that the matter of fact is so strong against them, that from the general propensity to pity the unfortunate, we express that sensation by the word *humanity* as if it was inseperable from our nature. That it is not *inseparable*, I have allowed in the former part of this discourse, from some reproachful instances of selfish tempers, which seem to take part in nothing beyond themselves; yet I am persuaded and affirm 'tis still so great and noble a part of our nature, that a man must do great violence to himself, and suffer many a painful conflict, before he has brought himself to a different disposition.

'Tis observable in the foregoing account, that when the priest came to the place where he was, he passed by on the other side—he might have passed by, you'll say, without turning aside.—No, there is a secret shame which attends every act of inhumanity not to be conquered in the hardest natures, so that, as in other cases, so especially in this, many a man will do a cruel act, who at the same time will blush to look you in the face, and is forced to turn aside before he can have the heart to execute his purpose.

Inconsistent creature that a man is! who at that instant that he does what is wrong, is not able to withold his testimony to what is good and praise worthy.

I have now done with the parable, which was the first part proposed to be considered in this discourse; and should proceed to the second, which so naturally falls from it, of exhorting you, as our SAVIOUR did the lawyer upon it, *to go and do so likewise*: but I have been so copious in my reflections upon the story itself, that I find I have insensibly incorporated into them almost all that I should have said here in recommending so amiable an example; by which means I have unawares anticipated the talk I proposed. I shall therefore detain you no longer than with a single remark upon the subject in general, which is this, 'Tis observable in many places of the scripture, that our blessed SAVIOUR in describing the day of judgement does it in such a manner, as if the great enquiry then, was to relate principally to this one virtue of compassion—and as if our final sentence at that solemnity was to be pronounced exactly according to the degrees of it. I was a hungred and ye gave me meat—thirsty and ye gave me drink—naked and ye clothed me—I was sick and ye visited me—in prison and ye came unto me.[1] Not that we are to imagine from thence, as if any other good or evil action should then be overlooked by the eye of the All-seeing Judge, but barely to intimate to us, that a charitable and benevolent disposition is so principal and ruling a part of a man's character, as to be a considerable test by itself of the whole frame and temper of his mind, with which all other virtues and vices respectively rise and fall, and will almost necessarily be connected.—Tell me therefore of a compassionate man, you represent to me a man of a thousand other good qualities— on whom I can depend—whom I may safely trust with my wife—my children, my fortune and reputation. 'Tis for this, as the apostle argues from the same principle—that he will not commit adultery— that he will not kill—that he will not steal—that he will not bear false witness. That is, the sorrows which are stirred up in men's hearts by such trespasses are so tenderly felt by a compassionate man, that it is not in his power or his nature to commit them.

So that well might he conclude, that charity, by which he means, the love to your neighbor, was the end of the commandment, and whosoever fulfilled it, had fulfilled the law.

Now to God, &c. Amen.

[1] *Matthew* XXV, 35, 36.

Sermon IV
SELF-KNOWLEDGE[1]

2 Samuel XII. 7 (1st part).
And Nathan said unto David thou art the man.

THERE IS no historical passage in scripture, which gives a more remarkable instance of deceitfulness of the heart of man to itself, and of how little we truly know ourselves, than this, wherein David is convicted out of his own mouth, and is led by the prophet to condemn and pronounce a severe judgement upon another, for an act of injustice, which he had passed over in himself, and possibly reconciled to his own conscience. To know one's self, one would think could be no very difficult lesson;—for who, you'll say, can well be truly ignorant of himself and the true disposition of his own heart. If a man thinks at all, he cannot be a stranger to what passes there—he must be conscious of his own thoughts and desires, he must remember his past pursuits, and the true springs and motives which in general have directed the actions of his life: he may hang out false colours and deceive the world, but how can a man deceive himself? That a man can—is evident, because he daily does so.—Scripture tells us, and gives us many historical proofs of it, besides this to which the text refers—that the heart of man is treacherous to itself and *deceitful above all things*;[2] and experience and every hour's commerce with the world confirms the truth of this

[1] Many of the ideas in this sermon are derivative from Butler (see Joseph Butler 'Upon Self-Deceit') and Swift (see Jonathan Swift, 'The Difficulty of Knowing One's Self').
[2] *Jeremiah*, XVII, 9.

seeming paradox, 'That though man is the only creature endowed with reflection, and consequently qualified to know the most of himself—yet so it happens, that he generally knows the least—and with all the power which GOD has given him of turning his eyes inwards upon himself, and taking notice of the chain of his own thoughts and desires—yet in fact, is generally so inattentive, but always so partial an observer of what passes, that he is as much, nay often, a much greater stranger to his own disposition and true character than all the world besides.'[1]

By what means he is brought under so manifest a delusion, and how he suffers himself to be so grossly imposed upon in a point which he is capable of knowing so much better than others, is not hard to give an account of, nor need we seek further for it, than amongst the causes which are every day perverting his reason and misleading him. We are deceived in judging of ourselves, just as we are in judging of other things, when our passions and inclinations are called in as counsellors, and we suffer ourselves to see and reason just so far and no farther than they give us leave. How hard do we find it to pass an equitable and sound judgement in a matter where our interest is deeply concerned?—and even where there is the remotest consideration of self, connected with the point before us, what a strange bias does it hang upon our minds, and how difficult is it to disengage our judgements entirely from it? with what reluctance are we brought to think evil of a friend whom we have long loved and esteemed, and though there happens to be strong appearances against him, how apt are we to overlook or put favourable constructions upon them, and even sometimes, when our zeal and friendship transport us, to assign the best and kindest motives for the worst and most unjustifiable parts of his conduct.

We are still worse casuists, and the deceit is proportionably stronger with a man, when he is going to judge of himself—that dearest of all parties,—so closely connected with him—so much and

[1] This passage is marked as a quotation, but it is actually a paraphrase from Swift (see note 1) '. . . and to shew whence it comes to pass that man, the only creature in the world that can reflect and look into himself, should know so little of what passeth within him, and be so very much unacquainted even with the standing dispositions and complexions of his own heart.'

so long beloved—of whom he has so early conceived the highest opinion and esteem, and with whose merit he has all along, no doubt, found so much reason to be contented. It is not an easy matter to be severe, where there is such an impulse to be kind, or to efface at once all the tender impressions in favour of so old a friend, which disable us from thinking of him, as he is, and seeing him in the light, may be, in which every one else sees him.

So that however easy this knowledge of one's-self may appear at first sight, it is otherwise when we come to examine; since not only in practice but even in speculation and theory, we find it one of the hardest and most painful lessons. Some of the earliest instructors of mankind, no doubt, found it so too, and for that reason, soon saw the necessity of laying such stress upon this great precept of self knowledge, which for its excellent wisdom and usefulness, many of them supposed to be a divine direction; that it came down from Heaven, and comprehended the whole circle both of the knowledge and the duty of man. And indeed their zeal might easily be allowed in so high an encomium upon the attainment of a virtue, the want of which so often baffled their instructions, and rendered their endeavors of reforming the heart vain and useless. For who could think of a reformation of the faults without him, who knew not where they lay, or could set about correcting, till he had first come to a sense of the defects which required it.

But this was a point always much easier recommended by public instructors than shewn how to be put in practice, and therefore others, who equally sought the reformation of mankind, observing that this direct road which led to it was guarded on all sides by self-love, and consequently very difficult to open access, soon found out a different and more artful course was requisite; as they had not strength to remove this flattering passion which stood in their way and blocked up all the passages to the heart, they endeavoured by stratagem to get beyond it, and by a skilful address, if possible, to deceive it. This gave rise to the early manner of conveying their instructions in parables, fables, and such sort of indirect applications, which tho' they could not conquer this principle of self-love, yet it often laid it asleep, or at least over-reached it for a few moments, till a just judgement could be procured.

The prophet Nathan seems to have been a great master in this way of address. David had greatly displeased G o d by two grievous sins which he had committed, and the prophet's commission was to go and bring him to a conviction of them, and touch his heart with a sense of guilt for what he had done against the honour and life of Uriah.

The holy man knew, that was it any one's case but David's own, no man would have been so quick-sighted in discerning the nature of the injury,—more ready to have redressed it, or who would have felt more compassion for the party who had suffered it, than he himself.

Instead therefore of declaring the real intention of his errand, by a direct accusation and reproof for the crimes he had committed; he comes to him with a fictitious complaint of a cruel act of injustice done by another, and accordingly he frames a case, not so parallel to David's as he supposed would awaken his suspicion, and prevent a patient and candid hearing, and yet not so void of resemblance in the main circumstances, as to fail of striking him when shewn in a proper light.

And Nathan came and said unto him, 'There were two men in one city, the one rich and the other poor—the rich man had exceeding many flocks and herds, but the poor man had nothing, save one little ewe lamb which he had bought and nourished up—and it grew up together with him and with his children—it did eat of his own meat, and drank of his own cup, and lay in his bosom, and was unto him as a daughter—and there came a traveller unto the rich man, and he spared to take of his own flock and of his own herd to dress for the wayfaring man that was come unto him, but took the poor man's lamb and dressed it for the man that was come unto him.'

The case was drawn with great judgment and beauty—the several minute circumstances which heightened the injury truly affecting—and so strongly urged, that it would have been impossible for any man with a previous sense of guilt upon his mind, to have defended himself from some degree of remorse, which it must naturally have excited.

The story, though it spoke only of the injustice and oppressive act of another man—yet it pointed to what he had lately done himself, with all the circumstances of its aggravation—and withal, the whole was so tenderly addressed to the heart and passions, as to kindle at once the utmost horror and indignation. And so it did,—but not against the proper person. In his transport he forgot himself—his anger greatly kindled against the man—and he said unto Nathan, 'As the Lord liveth, the man that hath done this thing shall surely die, and he shall restore the lamb fourfold, because he did this thing and because he had no pity.'

It can scarce be doubted here, but that David's anger was *real*, and that he was what he appeared to be, greatly provoked and exasperated against the offender: and, indeed, his sentence against him proves he was so above measure. For to punish the man with death, and oblige him to restore fourfold besides, was highly unequitable, and not only disproportioned to the offence, but far above the utmost rigour and severity of the law, which allowed a much softer atonement, requiring in such a case, no more than an ample restitution and recompense in kind. The judgement however, seems to have been truly sincere and well-meant, and bespoke rather the honest rashness of an unsuspicious judge, than the cool determination of a conscious and guilty man, who knew he was going to pass sentence upon himself.

I take notice of this particular, because it places this instance of self deceit, which is the subject of the discourse, in the strongest light, and fully demonstrates the truth of a fact in this great man, which happens every day amongst ourselves, namely, that a man may be guilty of very bad and dishonest actions, and yet reflect so little, or so partially, upon what he has done, as to keep his conscience free, not only from guilt, but even the remotest suspicions, that he is the man which in truth he is, and what the tenor and evidence of his life demonstrate. If we look into the world—David's is no uncommon case—we see some one or other perpetually copying this bad original, sitting in judgement upon himself—hearing his own cause, and not knowing what he is doing; hasty in passing sentence, and even executing it too with wrath upon the person of another, when in the language of the prophet, one might say to him with justice, 'thou art the man.'

Of the many revengeful, covetous, false and ill-natured persons which we complain of in the world, though we all join in the cry against them, what man amongst us singles out himself as a criminal, or ever once takes it into his head that he adds to the number ?—

or where is there a man so bad, who would not think it the hardest and most unfair imputation to have any of those particular vices laid to his charge?

If he has the symptoms never so strong upon him, which he would pronounce infallible in another, they are indications of no such malady in himself.—He sees what no one else sees, some secret and flattering circumstances in his favour, which no doubt make a wide difference betwixt his case and the parties which he condemns.

What other man speaks so often and vehemently against the vice of pride, sets the weakness of it in a more odious light, or is more hurt with it in another, than the proud man himself? It is the same with the passionate, the designing, the ambitious, and some other common characters in life; and being a consequence of the nature of such vices, and almost inseperable from them, the effects of it are generally so gross and absurd, that where pity does not forbid, 'tis pleasant to observe and trace the cheat through the several turns and windings of the heart, and detect it through all the shapes and appearances which it puts on.

Next to these instances of self deceit and utter ignorance of our true disposition and character, which appears in not seeing *that* in ourselves which shocks us in another man, there is another species still more dangerous and delusive, and which the more guarded perpetually fall into from the judgements they make of different vices, according to their age and complexion, and the various ebbs and flows of their passions and desires.

To conceive this, let any man look into his own heart, and observe in how different a degree of detestation, numbers of actions stand there, though equally bad and vicious in themselves: he will soon find that such of them, as strong inclination or custom has prompted him to commit, are generally dressed out, and painted with all the false beauties which a soft and flattering hand can give them; and that the others, to which he feels no propensity, appear at once naked and deformed, surrounded with all the true circumstances of their folly and dishonour.

When David surprised Saul sleeping in the cave, and cut off the skirt of his robe, we read, his heart smote him for what he had done;[1]—strange! it smote him not in the matter of Uriah, where it

[1] I *Samuel*, XXIV, 4, 5.

had so much stronger reason to take the alarm.—A whole year had almost passed from the first commission of that injustice, to the time the prophet was sent to reprove him—and we read not once of any remorse or compunction of heart for what he had done: and it is not to be doubted, had the same prophet met him when he was returning up out of the cave—and told him, that scrupulous and conscientious as he then seemed and thought himself to be, that he was deceiving himself, and was capable of committing the foulest and most dishonourable actions;—that he should one day murder a faithful and a valiant servant, whom he ought in justice to have loved and honoured,—that he should without pity first wound him in the tenderest part, by taking away his dearest possession,—and then unmercifully and treacherously rob him of his life.—Had Nathan in a prophetic spirit foretold to David that he was capable of this, and that he should one day actually do it, and from no other motive but the momentary gratification of a base and unworthy passion, he would have received the prediction with horror, and said possibly with Hazael upon just such another occasion, and with the same ignorance of himself—*What? is thy servant a dog that he should do this great thing?*[1] And yet in all likelihood, at that very time there wanted nothing but the same degree of temptation, and the same opportunity, to induce him to the sin which afterwards overcame him.

Thus the case stands with us still. When the passions are warmed, and the sin which presents itself exactly tallies to the desire, observe how impetuously a man will rush into it, and act against all principles of honour, justice and mercy.—Talk to him the moment after upon the nature of another vice to which he is not addicted, and from which perhaps his age, his temper, or rank in life secure him—take notice, how well he reasons—with what equity he determines—what an honest indignation and sharpness he expresses against it, and how insensibly his anger kindles against a man who hath done this thing.

Thus we are nice in grains and scruples—but knaves in matters of a pound weight—every day straining at gnats, yet swallowing camels—miserably cheating ourselves, and torturing our reason to

[1] II *Kings,* VIII, 13.

bring us in such a report of the sin as suits the present appetite and inclination.

Most of us are aware of and pretend to detest the barefaced instances of that hypocrisy by which men deceive others, but few of us are upon our guard or see that more fatal hypocrisy by which we deceive and over-reach our own hearts. It is a flattering and dangerous distemper, which has undone thousands—we bring the seeds of it along with us into the world—they insensibly grow up with us from childhood—they lye long concealed and undisturbed, and have generally got such deep root in our natures by the time we are come to years of understanding and reflection, that it requires all we have got to defend ourselves from their effects.

To make the case still worse on our sides, 'tis with this as with every grievous distemper of the body—the remedies are dangerous and doubtful, in proportion to our mistakes and ignorance of the cause: for in the instances of self-deceit, though the head is sick, and the whole heart faint, the patient seldom knows what he ails:—of all things we know and learn, this necessary knowledge comes to us the last.

Upon what principles it happens thus, I have endeavoured to lay open in the first part of this discourse; which I conclude with a serious exhortation to struggle against them; which we can only hope to do, by conversing more and oftener with ourselves, than the business and diversions of the world generally give us leave.

We have a chain of thoughts, desires, engagements, and idlenesses, which perpetually return upon us in their proper time and order,—let us, I beseech you, assign and set apart some small portion of the day for this purpose—of retiring unto ourselves, and searching into the dark corners and recesses of the heart, and taking notice of what is passing there. If a man can bring himself to do this task with a curious and impartial eye, he will quickly find the fruits of it will more than recompense his time and labour. He will see several irregularities and unsuspected passions within him which he never was aware of,—he will discover in his progress many secret turns and windings in his heart to which he was a stranger, which now gradually open and disclose themselves to him upon a nearer view; in these labyrinths he will trace out such hidden springs and motives for many of his most applauded actions, as will make him rather sorry, and ashamed of himself, than proud.

In a word, he will understand *his errors*, and then see the necessity, with David, of imploring GOD to cleanse him from his secret faults—and with some hope and confidence to say, with this great man after his conviction—'Try me, O God! and seek the ground of my heart,—prove me and examine my thoughts, look well if there be any way of wickedness in me, and lead me in the way everlasting.'[1]

Now to God the father, &c. &c.

[1] Psalm 139, 23, 24.

Sermon X
JOB'S ACCOUNT OF THE SHORTNESS AND TROUBLES OF LIFE CONSIDERED

Job XIV. 1, 2.
Man that is born of a woman, is of few days, and full of trouble:—He cometh forth like a flower, and is cut down; he fleeth also as a shadow, and continueth not.

THERE IS something in this reflection of holy Job's, upon the shortness of life, and instability of human affairs, so beautiful and truly sublime; that one might challenge the writings of the most celebrated orators of antiquity, to produce a specimen of eloquence, so noble and thoroughly affecting. Whether this effect be owing in some measure, to the pathetic nature of the subject reflected on; or to the eastern manner of expression, in a style more exalted and suitable to so great a subject, or (which is the more likely account,) because they are properly the words of that being, who first inspired man with language, and taught his mouth to utter, who opened the lips of the dumb, and made the tongue of the infant eloquent;— to which of these we are to refer the beauty and sublimity of this, as well as that of numberless other passages of the holy writ, may not seem now material; but surely without these helps, never man was better qualified to make just and noble reflections upon the shortness of life, and instability of human affairs, than Job was, who had himself waded through such a sea of troubles, and in his passage had encountered many vicissitudes of storms and sunshine, and by turns had felt both the extremes, of all the happiness, and all the wretchedness that mortal man is heir to.

The beginning of his days was crowned with every thing that ambition could wish for;—he was the greatest of all the men of the East,—had large and unbounded possessions, and no doubt enjoyed all the comforts and advantages of life, which they could administer.—Perhaps you will say a wise man might not be inclined to give a full loose to this kind of happiness, without some better security for the support of it, than the mere possession of such goods of fortune, which often slip from under us, and sometimes unaccountably make themselves wings, and fly away.—But he had that security too,—for the hand of providence which had thus far protected, was still leading him forwards, and seemed engaged in the preservation and continuance of these blessings;—God had set a hedge about him, and about all that he had on every side, he had blessed all the works of his hands, and his substance increased every day. Indeed even with this security, riches to him that hath *neither child or brother*, as the wise man observes, instead of a comfort prove sometimes a sore travel and vexation.—The mind of man is not always satisfied with the reasonable assurance of its own enjoyments, but will look forwards, as if it discovers some imaginary void, the want of some beloved object to fill his place after him, will often disquiet itself in vain, and say—'For whom do I labour, and bereave myself of rest?'[1]

This bar to his happiness God had likewise taken away, in blessing him with a numerous offspring of sons and daughters, the apparent inheritors of all his present happiness.—Pleasing reflection! to think the blessings God has indulged one's self in, shall be handed and continued down to a man's own seed; how little does this differ from a second enjoyment of them, to an affectionate parent, who naturally looks forward with as strong an interest upon his children, as if he was to live over again in his own posterity.

What could be wanting to finish such a picture of a happy man?—Surely nothing, except a virtuous disposition to give a relish to these blessings, and direct him to make a proper use of them.—He had that too, for he was a perfect and upright man, one that feared God and eschewed evil.

In the midst of all this prosperity, which was as great as could

[1] *Ecclesiastes*, IV, 8.

well fall to the share of one man;—whilst all the world looked gay, and smiled upon him, and every thing round him seemed to promise, if possible, an increase of happiness, in one instant all is changed into sorrow and utter despair.—

It pleased God for wise purposes to blast the fortunes of his house, and cut off all hopes of his posterity, and in one mournful day to bring this great prince from his palace down to the dunghill. His flocks and herds, in which consisted the abundance of his wealth, were part consumed by a fire from heaven, the remainder taken away by the sword of the enemy: his sons and daughters, whom 'tis natural to imagine so good a man had so brought up in a sense of their duty, as to give him all reasonable hopes of much joy and pleasure in their future lives;—natural prospect for a parent to look forwards at, to recompense him for the many cares and anxieties which their infancy had cost him! these dear pledges of his future happiness were all, all snatched from him at one blow, just at that time that one might imagine they were beginning to be the comfort and delight of his old age, which most wanted such staves to lean on;—and as circumstances add to an evil, so they did to this;—for it fell out not only by a very calamitous accident, which was grievous enough in itself, but likewise upon the back of his other misfortunes, when he was ill prepared to bear such a shock; and what would still add to it, it happened at an hour when he had least reason to expect it, when he would naturally think his children secure and out of the way of danger. 'For whilst they were feasting and making merry in their eldest brother's house, a great wind out of the wilderness smote the four corners of the house, and it fell upon them.'

Such a concurrence of misfortunes are not the common lot of many: and yet there are instances of some who have undergone as severe trials, and bravely struggled under them; perhaps by natural force of spirits, the advantages of health, and the cordial assistance of a friend. And with these helps, what may not a man sustain?—But this was not Job's case; for scarce had these evils fallen upon him, when he was not only borne down with a grievous distemper which afflicted him from the crown of his head to the soul of his foot, but likewise his three friends, in whose kind consolations he might have found a medicine,—even the wife of his bosom, whose duty it was with a gentle hand to have softened all his sorrows, instead of

77

doing this, they cruelly insulted and became the reproachers of his integrity. O God! what is man when thou thus bruisest him, and maketh his burthen heavier as his strength grows less?—Who, that had found himself thus an example of the many changes and chances of this mortal life;—when he considered himself now stripped and left destitute of so many valuable blessings which the moment before thy providence had poured upon his head;—when he reflected upon this gay delightsome structure, in appearance so strongly built, so pleasingly surrounded with every thing that could flatter his hopes and wishes, and beheld it all levelled with the ground in one moment, and the whole prospect vanish with it like the description of an enchantment;—who I say that had seen and felt the shock of so sudden a revolution, would not have been furnished with just and beautiful reflections upon the occasion, and said with Job in the words of the text, 'That man is born of a woman, is of few days, and full of misery—that he cometh forth like a flower, and is cut down; he fleeth also as a shadow and continueth not?'

The words of the text are an epitome of the *natural* and *moral* vanity of man, and contain two distinct declarations concerning his state and condition in each respect.

First, that he is a creature of few days; and secondly, that those days are full of trouble.

I shall make some reflections upon each of these in their order, and conclude with a practical lesson from the whole.

And first, that he is of few days. The comparison which Job makes use of, That man cometh forth like a flower, is extremely beautiful, and more to the purpose than the most elaborate proof, which in truth the subject will not easily admit of;—the shortness of life being a point so generally complained of in all ages since the flood, and so universally felt and acknowledged by the whole species, as to require no evidence beyond a similitude; the intent of which is not so much to prove the fact, as to illustrate and place it in such a light as to strike us, and bring the impression home to ourselves in a more affecting manner.

Man comes forth, says Job, like a flower, and is cut down;—he is sent into the world the fairest and noblest part of God's works—fashioned after the image of his creator with respect to reason and the great faculties of the mind; he cometh forth glorious as the flower of the field; as it surpasses the vegetable world in beauty, so does he the animal world in the glory and excellencies of his nature.

The one—if no untimely accident oppress it, soon arrives at the full period of its perfection,—is suffered to triumph for a few moments, and is plucked up by the roots in the very pride and gayest stage of its being:—or if it happens to escape the hands of violence, in a few days it necessarily sickens of itself and dies away.

Man likewise, though his progress is slower, and his duration something longer, yet the periods of his growth and declension are nearly the same both in the nature and manner of them.

If he escapes the dangers which threaten his tenderer years, he is soon got into the full maturity and strength of life; and if he is so fortunate as not to be hurried out of it then by accidents, by his own folly and intemperance—if he escapes these, he naturally decays himself;—a period comes fast upon him, beyond which he was not made to last.—Like a flower or fruit which may be plucked up by force before the time of their maturity, yet cannot be made to outgrow the period when they are to fade and drop themselves; when that comes, the hand of nature then plucks them both off, and no art of the botanist can uphold the one, or skill of the physician preserve the other, beyond periods to which their original frames and constitutions were made to extend. As God has appointed and determined the several growths and decays of the vegetable race, so he seems as evidently to have prescribed the same laws to man, as well as all living creatures, in the first rudiments of which, there are contained the specific powers of their growth, duration and extinction; and when the evolutions of those animal powers are exhausted and run down, the creature expires and dies of itself, as ripe fruit falls from a tree, or a flower preserved beyond its bloom drops and perishes upon the stalk.

Thus much for this comparison of Job's, which though it is very poetical, yet conveys a just idea of the thing referred to.—'That he fleeth also as a shadow, and continueth not'—is no less a faithful and fine representation of the shortness and vanity of human life, of which one cannot give a better explanation, than by referring to the original, from whence the picture was taken.—With how quick a succession, do days, months and years pass over our heads?—how truely like a shadow that departeth do they flee away insensibly, and scarce leave an impression with us?—when we endeavour to call them back by reflection, and consider in what manner they have gone, how unable are the best of us to give a tolerable account?—and were it not for some of the more remarkable stages which have distinguished a few periods of this rapid progress—we should look back upon it all as Nebuchadnezzar did upon his dream when he awoke in the morning;—he was sensible many things had passed, and troubled him too; but had passed on so quickly, they had left no footsteps behind, by which he could be enabled to trace them back.—Melancholy account of the life of man! which generally runs on in such a manner, as scarce to allow time to make reflections which way it has gone.

How many of our first years slide by, in the innocent sports of childhood, in which we are not able to make reflections upon them? —how many more thoughtless years escape us in our youth, when we are unwilling to do it, and are so eager in the pursuit of pleasure as to have no time to spare, to stop and consider them?

When graver and riper years come on, and we begin to think it time to reform and set up for men of sense and conduct, then the business and perplexing interests of this world, and the endless plotting and contriving how to make the most of it, do so wholly employ us, that we are too busy to make reflections upon so unprofitable a subject.—As families and children increase, so do our affections, and with them are multiplied our cares and toils for their preservation and establishment;—all which take up our thoughts so closely, and possess them so long, that we are often overtaken by grey hairs before we see them, or have found leisure to consider how far we were got,—what we have been doing,—and for what purpose God sent us into the world. As man may justly be said to be of few days considered with respect to this hasty succession of things, which soon carries him into the decline of his life, so may he likewise be said to flee like a shadow and continue not, when his duration is compared with other parts of God's works, and even the works of his own hands, which outlast him many generations;—whilst his—as Homer observes, like leaves, one generation drops, and another springs up to fall again and be forgotten.

But when we farther consider his days in the light in which we ought chiefly to view them, as they appear in thy sight, O God! with whom a thousand years are but as yesterday; when we reflect that this hand-breadth of life is all that is measured out to us from that eternity for which he is created, how does his short span vanish to nothing in the comparison? 'Tis true, the greatest portion of time will do the same when compared with what is to come; and therefore so short and transitory a one, as threescore years and ten, beyond which all is declared to be labour and sorrow, may the easier be allowed: and yet how uncertain are we of that portion, short as it is? Do not ten thousand accidents break off the slender thread of human life, long before it can be drawn out to that extent? —The new-born babe falls down an easy prey, and moulders back again into dust, like a tender blossom put forth in an untimely hour. —The hopeful youth in the very pride and beauty of life is cut off, some cruel distemper or unthought of accident lays him prostrate upon the earth, to pursue Job's comparison, like a blooming flower smit and shrivelled up with a malignant blast.—In this stage of life chances multiply upon us,—the seeds of disorders are sown by intemperance or nelgect,—infectious distempers are more easily contracted, when contracted they rage with greater violence, and the success in many cases is more doubtful, insomuch that they who have exercised themselves in computations of this kind tell us, 'That one half of the whole species which are born into the world, go out of it again, and are all dead in so short a space as the fiist seventeen years.'[1]

These reflections may be sufficient to illustrate the first part of Job's declaration, *'That man is of few days.'* Let us examine the truth of the other, and see, whether he is not likewise full of trouble.

And here we must not take our account from the flattering outside of things, which are generally set off with a glittering appearance enough, especially in what is called, *higher life.*—Nor can we safely trust the evidence of some of the more merry and thoughtless

[1] Sterne could have discovered a statistic such as this from any one of several sources. Most probably he had the information from the only partially reliable compilation of births and deaths derived from parish registers. A head count census was not undertaken in Britain until 1801.

amongst us, who are so set upon the enjoyment of life as seldom to reflect upon the troubles of it;—or who, perhaps, because they are not yet come to this portion of their inheritance, imagine it is not their common lot.—Nor lastly, are we to form an idea of it, from the delusive stories of a few of the most prosperous passengers, who have fortunately sailed through and escaped the rougher toils and distresses. But we are to take our accounts from a close survey of human life, and the real face of things, stript of every thing that can palliate or gild it over. We must hear the general complaint of all ages, and read the histories of mankind. If we look into them, and examine them to the bottom, what do they contain but the history of sad and uncomfortable passages, which a good-natured man cannot read but with oppression of spirits.—Consider the dreadful succession of wars in one part or other of the earth, perpetuated from one century to another with so little intermission, that mankind have scarce had time to breathe from them, since ambition first came into the world; consider the horrid effects of them in all those barbarous devastations we read of, where whole nations have been put to the sword, or have been driven out to nakedness and famine to make room for newcomers. For a specimen of this, let us reflect upon the story related by Plutarch, when by order of the Roman senate, seventy populous cities were unawares sacked and destroyed at one prefixed hour, by P. Æmilius, by whom one hundred and fifty thousand unhappy people were driven into captivity, to be sold to the highest bidder to end their days in cruel anguish.[1]
—Consider how great a part of our species in all ages down to this, have been trod under the feet of cruel and capricious tyrants, who would neither hear their cries, nor pity their distresses,—Consider slavery—what it is,—how bitter a draught, and how many millions have been made to drink of it;—which if it can poison all earthly happiness when exercised barely upon our bodies, what must it be, when it comprehends both the slavery of body and mind?—To conceive this, look into the history of the Romish church and her tyrants, (or rather executioners) who seem to have taken pleasure in the pangs and convulsions of their fellow creatures.—Examine the prisons of the inquisition, hear the melancholy notes sounded in

[1] The example of Plutarch was omitted in later editions of the *Sermons*. Sterne had used it already in Sermon IX, Volume II.

every cell.—Consider the anguish of mock-trials, and the exquisite tortures consequent thereupon, mercilessly inflicted upon the unfortunate, where the racked and weary soul has so often wished to take its leave,—but cruelly not suffered to depart.—Consider how many of these helpless wretches have been haled from thence in all periods of this tyrannic usurpation, to undergo the massacres and flames to which a false and a bloody religion has condemned them. If this sad history and detail of the more public causes of the miseries of man are not sufficient, let us behold him in another light with respect to the more private causes of them, and see whether he is not full of trouble likewise there, and almost born to it as naturally as the sparks fly upwards. If we consider man as a creature of wants and necessities (whether real or imaginary) which he is not able to supply of himself, what a train of disappointments, vexations and dependencies are apt to be seen, issuing from thence to perplex and make his being uneasy?—How many justlings and hard struggles do we undergo, in making our way in the world?—How barbarously held back?—How often and basely overthrown, in aiming only at getting bread?—How many of us never attain it—at least not comfortably,—but from various unknown causes—eat it all our lives long in bitterness?

If we shift the scene, and look upwards, towards those whose situation in life seems to place them above the sorrows of this kind, yet where are they exempt from others? Do not all ranks and conditions of men meet with sad accidents and numberless calamities in other respects which often make them go heavily all their lives long?

How many fall into chronical infirmities, which render both their days and nights restless and insupportable?—How many of the highest rank are tore up with ambition, or soured with disappointments, and how many more from a thousand secret causes of disquiet pine away in silence, and owe their deaths to sorrow and dejection of the heart?—If we cast our eyes upon the lowest class and condition of life,—the scene is more melancholy still.—Millions of our fellow-creatures, born to no inheritance but poverty and trouble, forced by the necessity of their lots to drudgery and painful employments, and hard set with that too, to get enough to keep themselves and families alive.—So that upon the whole, when we have examined the true state and condition of human life, and have made some allowances for the few fugacious, deceitful pleasures, there is scarce any thing to be found which contradicts Job's description of it. —Which ever way we look abroad, we see some legible characters of what GOD first denounced against us, 'That in sorrow we should eat our bread, till we return to the ground from whence we were taken.'*

But some one will say, Why are we thus to be put out of love with human life? To what purpose is it to expose the dark sides of it to us, or enlarge upon the infirmities which are natural, and consequently out of our power to redress?

I answer, that the subject is nevertheless of great importance, since it is necessary every creature should understand his present state and condition, to put him in mind of behaving suitably to it.— Does not an impartial survey of man—the holding up this glass to shew him his defects and natural infirmities, naturally tend to cure his pride and cloath him with humility, which is a dress that best becomes a short-lived and a wretched creature?—Does not the consideration of the shortness of our life convince us of the wisdom of dedicating so small a portion to the great purposes of eternity?—

Lastly, When we reflect that this span of life, short as it is, is chequered with so many troubles, that there is nothing in this world springs up, or can be enjoyed without a mixture of sorrow, how insensibly does it incline us to turn our eyes and affections from so gloomy a prospect, and fix them upon that happier country, where afflictions cannot follow us, and where GOD will wipe away all the tears from off our faces for ever and ever? Amen.

* N.B. Most of these reflections upon the miseries of life are taken from Woollaston.

Sermon XVII

THE CASE OF HEZEKIAH AND THE MESSENGERS[1]

2 Kings XX. 15.

And Hezekiah said unto the Prophet, I have shewn them my vessels of silver, and my wives and my concubines, and my boxes of ointment, and whatever I have in my house, have I shewn unto them: and the Prophet said unto Hezekiah, thou hast done very foolishly.[2]

AND WHERE was the harm, you'll say, in all this? An eastern prince, the son of Baladine, had sent messengers with presents as far as from Babylon, to congratulate Hezekiah upon the recovery

[1] Sermon II in Vol. III. The title page of the first edition reads 'preached 1763 before the Earl of Hertford.' The date was actually 1764. Sterne was asked to speak at the dedication of a new chapel at the British Embassy in Paris, known to have been decorated with unprecedented lavishness. He wrote to a friend in July 1764 '. . . that unlucky kind of fit seized me, which you know I can never resist, and a very unlucky text did come into my head,—and you will say so when you read it.' This is known to be one of the last sermons Sterne ever delivered. He requested leave of the archbishop of York later that year, explaining that public speaking severely strained his already weak lungs. Much of this sermon is based on a 'Contemplation' by Joseph Hall, Bishop of Exeter.

[2] Sterne is paraphrasing and expanding here. The text reads 'And he said, what have they seen in thine house? And Hezekiah answered, All the things that are in mine house have they seen: there is nothing among my treasures that I have not shewed them.' Sterne adds information from verses 13 and 17 to the indicated chapter.

from his sickness; and Hezekiah, who was a good prince, acted consistently with himself: *he received and entertained the men and hearkened unto them,* and before he sent them away, he courteously shewed them all that was worth a stranger's curiosity in his house and in his kingdom—and in this, seemed only to have discharged himself of what urbanity or the *etiquette* of courts might require. Notwithstanding this, in the verse which immediately follows the text, we find he had done amiss; and as punishment for it, that all his riches, which his forefathers had laid up in store unto that day, were threatened to be carried away in triumph to Babylon,—the very place from whence the messengers had come.

A hard return! and what his behaviour does not seem to have deserved. To set this matter in a clear light, it will be necessary to enlarge upon the whole story,—the reflections which will arise out of it, as we go along, may help us—at least, I hope they will be of use on their own account.

After the miraculous defeat of the Assyrians, we read in the beginning of this chapter, that Hezekiah was sick even unto death; and that G o d sends the prophet Isaiah, with the unwelcome message, *that he should set his house in order, for that he should die, and not live.*

There are many instances of men, who have received such news with great ease of mind, and even entertained thoughts of it with smiles upon their countenances,—and this, either from strength of spirits and the natural chearfulness of their temper,—or that, they knew the world, and cared not for it,—or expected a better—yet thousands of good men with all the helps of philosophy, and against all the assurances of a well spent life, that the change must be to their account,—upon the approach of death have still lean'd towards this world, and wanted spirits and resolution to bear the shock of a separation from it for ever.

This in some measure seemed to have been Hezekiah's case; for tho' he had walked before G o d in truth, and with a perfect heart, and had done that which was good in his sight,—yet we find that the hasty summons afflicted him greatly;—that upon the delivery of the message he wept sore;—that he turned his face towards the wall,— perhaps for the greater secrecy of his devotion, and that, by withdrawing himself thus from all external objects, he might offer up his prayer unto his GOD, with greater and more fervent attention.

—And he pray'd, and said, O LORD! I beseech thee remember—O Hezekiah! How couldst thou fear that GOD had forgotten thee? or, How couldst thou doubt of his remembrance of thy integrity, when he called thee to receive its recompence?

But here it appears of what materials man is made: he pursues happiness—and yet is so content with misery, that he would wander for ever in this dark vale of it,—and say, '*It is good, Lord! to be here, and to build tabernacles of rest:*'[1] and so long as we are cloathed with flesh, and nature has so great a share within us, it is no wonder if that part claims its right, and pleads for the sweetness of life, notwithstanding all its care and disappointments.

This natural weakness, no doubt, had its weight in Hezekiah's earnest prayer for life: and yet from the success it met with, and the immediate change of GOD's purpose thereupon, it is hard to imagine, but that it must have been accompanied with some meritorious and more generous motive: and if we suppose, as some have done, that he turned his face towards the wall, because that part of his chamber looked towards the temple, the care of whose preservation lay next to his heart, we may consistently enough give this sense to his prayer.

'O God! remember how I have walked before thee in truth;—how much I have done to rescue thy religion from error and falsehood;—thou knowest that the eyes of the world are fixed upon me, as one that hath forsaken their idolatry, and restored thy worship;—that I stand in the midst of a crooked and corrupt generation, which looks thro' all my actions, and watches all events which happen to me: if now they shall see me snatched away in the midst of my days and service, How will thy great name suffer in my extinction? Will not the heathen say, This it is, to serve the GOD of Israel!—How faithfully did Hezekiah walk before him?—What enemies did he bring upon himself, in too warmly promoting his worship? and now when the hour of sickness and distress came upon him, and he most wanted the aid of his GOD:—behold how he was forsaken!'

It is not unreasonable, to ascribe some such pious and more disinterested motive to Hezekiah's desire of life, from the issue and

[1] Some sort of paraphrase of *Mark* IX, 5 (parallel to *Matthew* XVII, 4 and *Luke* IX, 33).

success of his prayer:—*for it came to pass before Isaiah had gone out into the middle court, that the word of the Lord came to him, saying, Turn again and tell Hezekiah I have heard his prayer, I have seen his tears, and behold I will heal him.*

It was upon this occasion, as we read in the 12th verse of this chapter, that Baradock-baladon, son of Baladine king of Babylon, sent letters and a present unto Hezekiah: he had heard the fame of his sickness and recovery; for as the Chaldeans were great searchers into the secrets of nature, especially into the motions of the celestial bodies, in all probability they had taken notice at that distance, of the strange appearance of the shadow's returning ten degrees backwards upon their dials, and had inquired and learned upon what account, and in whose favour, such a sign was given; so that this astronomical miracle, besides the political motive which it would suggest of courting such a favourite of heaven, had been sufficient by itself to have led a curious people as far as Jerusalem, that they might see the man for whose sake the sun had forsook his course.

And here we see how hard it is to stand the shock of prosperity,—and how much truer a proof we give of our strength in that extreme of life, than in the other.

In all the trials of adversity, we find that Hezekiah behaved well,—nothing unman'd him: when besieged by the Assyrian host, which shut him up in Jerusalem, and threaten'd his destruction,—he stood unshaken and depended upon GOD's succour.—When cast down upon his bed of sickness, and threaten'd with death, he meekly turn'd his face towards the wall,—wept and pray'd, and depended upon GOD's mercy:—but no sooner does prosperity return upon him, and the messengers from a far country come to pay the flattering homage due to his greatness, and the extraordinary felicity of his life, but he turns giddy, and sinks under the weight of his good fortune, and with a transport unbecoming a wise man upon it, 'tis said, he hearken'd unto the men, and shew'd them all the house of his precious things, the silver and gold, the spices and the precious ointments, and all the house of his armour, and all that was found in his treasures; that there was nothing in his house, nor in his dominions, that Hezekiah shew'd them not: for tho' it is not expressly said here, (tho' it is in the parallel passage in Chronicles)[1]—nor is he

[1] *2 Chronicles* XXXII, 25, 26.

charged by the prophet that, he did this out of vanity and a weak transport of ostentation;—yet as we are sure, GOD could not be offended but where there was a real crime, we might reasonably conclude that this was his, and that he who searches into the heart of man, beheld that his was corrupted with the blessings he had given him; and that it was just to make what was the occasion of his pride, become the instrument of his punishment, by decreeing, that all the riches he had laid up in store until that day, should be carried away in triumph to Babylon, the very place from whence the messengers had come who had been eye-witness to his folly.

'O Hezekiah! How couldst thou provoke GOD to bring this judgement upon thee? How could thy spirit, all-meek and gentle as it was, have ever fallen into this snare? Were thy treasures rich as the earth—What! was thy heart so vain as to be lifted up therewith? Was not all that was valuable in the world—nay, was not heaven it-self almost at thy command whilst thou wast humble? and, How was it, that thou couldst barter away all this, for what was lighter than a bubble, and desecrate an action so full of courtesy and kind-ness as thine appeared to be, by suffering it to take its rise from so polluted a fountain?'

There is scarce any thing which the heart more unwillingly bears, than an analysis of this kind.

We are a strange compound; and something foreign from what charity would suspect, so eternally twists itself into what we do, that not only in momentous concerns, where interest lists under it all the powers of disguise,—but even in the most indifferent of our actions,—not worth a fallacy—by force of habit, we continue it: so that whatever a man is about,—observe him,—he stands arm'd inside and out with two motives; an ostensible one for the world,— and another which he reserves for his own private use;—this, you may say, the world has no concern with: it might have been so; but by obtruding the wrong motive upon the world, and stealing from it a character, instead of winning one;—we give it a right and a tempta-tion along with it, to inquire into the affair.

The motives of the one for doing it, are often little better than the others for deserving it. Let us see if some social virtue may not be extracted from the errors of both the one and the other.

VANITY bids all her sons to be generous and brave,—and her

daughters to be chaste and courteous.—But why do we want her instructions?—Ask the comedian who is taught a part he feels not—

Is it that the principles of religion want strength, or that the real passion for what is good and worthy will not carry us high enough?—GOD! thou knowest they carry us too high—we want not *to be*—but *to seem*—

Look out of your door,—take notice of that man: see what disquieting, intriguing and shifting, he is content to go through, merely to be thought a man of plain dealing:—three grains of honesty would save him all this trouble—alas! he has them not.—

Behold a second, under a shew of piety hiding the impurities of a debauched life:—he is just entering the house of GOD:—would he was more pure—or less pious:—but then he could not gain his point.

Observe a third going on almost in the same track,—with what an inflexible sanctity of deportment, he sustains himself as he advances:—every line in his face writes abstinence;—every stride looks like a check upon his desires: see, I beseech you, how he is cloak'd up with sermons, prayers, and sacraments; and so bemuffled with the externals of religion, that he has not a hand to spare for a wordly purpose;—he has armour at least—Why does he put it on? Is there no serving GOD without all this? Must the garb of religion be extended so wide to the danger of its rending?—Yes truly, or it will not hide the secret—and, What is that?

—That the saint has no religion at all.

—But here comes GENEROSITY; giving—not to a decayed artist—but to the arts and sciences themselves.—See,—*he builds not a chamber in the wall apart for the prophet*;[1] but whole schools and colleges for those who come after. LORD! how they will magnify his name!—'tis in capitals already; the first—the highest, in the gilded rent-roll of every hospital and asylum.—

—One honest tear shed in private over the unfortunate, is worth it all.

What a problematic set of creatures does simulation make us! Who would divine that all that anxiety and concern so visible in the airs of one half of that great assembly should arise from nothing

[1] refers to Elisha and the Shunnemite woman 2 *Kings* IV, 10.

else, but that the other half of it may think them to be men of consequence, penetration, parts and conduct?—What a noise amongst the
claimants about it? Behold *Humility*, out of mere pride,—and honesty, almost out of knavery:—*Chastity*, never once in harm's way,—
and courage, like a Spanish soldier upon an Italian stage—a
bladder full of wind.—

—Hark! that, the sound of that trumpet,—let not my soldier
run,—'tis some good Christian giving alms. O, Pity, thou
gentlest of human passions! soft and tender are thy notes, and ill
accord with so loud an instrument.

Thus something jars, and will for ever jar in these cases: im-
posture is all dissonance, let what master so ever of it, undertake the
part; let him harmonize and modulate it as he may, one tone will
contradict another; and whilst we have ears to hear, we shall distinguish it: 'tis truth only which is consistent and ever in harmony
with itself: it sits upon our lips, like the natural notes of some
melodies, ready to drop out, whether we will or no;—it racks no
invention to let ourselves alone,—and needs fear no critick, to
have the same excellency in the heart which appears in the action.

It is a pleasing allusion the scripture makes use of in calling us
sometimes a house, sometimes a temple, according to the more or
less exalted qualities of the spiritual guest which is lodged within
us: whether this is the precise ground of the distinction, I will not
affirm; but thus much may be said, that, if we are to be temples,
'tis truth and singleness of heart which must make the dedication:
'tis this which must first distinguish them from the unhallowed pile,
where dirty tricks and impositions are practised by the host upon the
traveller, who tarries but for a moment and returns not again.

We all take notice, how close and reserved people are; but we
do not take notice at the same time, that every one may have something to conceal, as well as ourselves; and that we are only marking
the distances and taking the measures of self-defence from each
other in the very instances we complain of: this is so true, that there
is scarce any character so rare, as a man of real open and generous
integrity—who carries his heart in his hand,—who says the thing he
thinks; and does the thing he pretends. Tho' no one can dislike the
character,—yet, Discretion generally shakes her head,—and the
world soon lets him into the reason.

'*O that I had in the wilderness a lodging of way-faring men! that I might leave such a people, and go from them.*'[1] Where is the man of a nice sense of truth and strong feelings, from whom the duplicity of the world has not at one time or other wrung the same wish; and where lies the wilderness to which some one has not fled, from the same melancholy impulse?

Thus much for those who give occasion to be thought ill of:—let us say a word or two unto those who take it.

But to avoid all common-place cant, as much as I can on this head,—I will forbear to say, because I do not think it,—that 'tis a breach of Christian charity to think or speak evil of our neighbor, &c.

—We cannot avoid it: our opinions must follow the evidence; and we are perpetually in such engagements and situations, that 'tis our duties to speak what our opinions are—but GOD forbid that this ever should be done but from its best motive—the sense of what is due to virtue, governed by discretion and the utmost fellow feeling: were we to go on otherwise, beginning with the great broad cloak of hypocrisy, and so down through all its little trimmings and facings, tearing away without mercy all that look'd seemly,—we should leave but a tatter'd world of it.

But I confine what I have to say to a character less equivocal, and which takes up too much room in the world: it is that of those, who from a general distrust of all that looks disinterested, finding nothing to blame in an action, and perhaps much to admire in it,— immediately fall foul upon its motives: *Does Job serve God for nought?* What a vile insinuation! besides, the question was not, whether Job was a rich or a poor man;—but, whether he was a man of integrity or no? and the appearances were strong on his side: indeed it might have been otherwise; it was possible Job might be insincere, and the devil took the advantage of the die for it.

It is a bad picture, and done by a terrible master, and yet we are always copying it. Does a man from real conviction of heart forsake his vices?—the position is not to be allowed,—no; his vices have forsaken him.

Does a pure virgin fear GOD and say her prayers:—she is in her climacterick.

[1] *Jeremiah* IX, 2.

Does humanity cloath and educate the unknown orphan?—Poverty! thou hast no genealogies:—see! is he not the father of the child? Thus do we rob heroes of the best part of their glory—their virtue. Take away the motive of the act, you take away, all that is worth having in it;—wrest it to ungenerous ends, you load the virtuous man who did it, with infamy;—undo it all—I beseech you: give him back his honour,—restore the jewel you have taken from him—replace him in the eye of the world—

—it is too late.

It is painful to utter reproaches which should come in here.—I will trust them with yourselves: in coming from that quarter, they will more naturally produce such fruits as will not set your teeth on edge—for they will be the fruits of love and goodwill, to the praise of G o d and the happiness of the world, which I wish.

Sermon XX
THE PRODIGAL SON[1]

Luke XV. 13.

And not many days after, the younger son gathered all he had together, and took his journey into a far country.—

I KNOW not whether the remark is to our honour or otherwise, that lessons of wisdom have never such power over us, as when they are wrought into the heart, through the groundwork of a story which engages the passions: Is it that we are like iron, and must first be heated before we can be wrought upon? or, Is the heart so in love with deceit, that where a true report will not reach it, we must cheat it with a fable, in order to come at truth?

Whether this parable of the prodigal (for so it is usually called) —is really such, or built upon some story known at that time in Jerusalem, is not much to the purpose; it is given us to enlarge upon, and turn to the best moral account we can.

'A certain man,' says our SAVIOUR, 'had two sons, and the younger of them said to his father, Give me the portion of goods which falls to me: and he divided unto them his substance. And not many days after, the younger son gathered all together, and took his journey into a far country, and there wasted his substance with riotous living.'

The account is short: the interesting and pathetic passages with which such a transaction would be necessarily connected, are left to be supplied by the heart:—the story is silent—but nature is not:— much kind advice, and many a tender expostulation would fall from the father's lips, no doubt, upon this occasion.

[1] Sermon V in Volume III.

He would dissuade his son from the folly of so rash an enterprise, by shewing him the dangers of the journey,—the inexperience of his age,—the hazards his life, his fortune, his virtue would run, without a guide, without a friend: he would tell him of the many snares and temptations which he had to avoid, or encounter at every step,—the pleasures which would solicit him in every luxurious court,—the little knowledge he could gain—except that of evil: he would speak of the seductions of women,—their charms—their poisons: —what hapless indulgences he might give way to, when far from restraint, and the check of giving his father pain.

The dissuasive would but inflame his desire.—

He gathers all together.—

—I see the picture of his departure:—the camels and asses loaden with his substance, detached on one side of the piece, and already on their way:—the prodigal son standing on the fore ground, with a forced sedateness, struggling against the fluttering movement of joy, upon his deliverance from restraint:—the elder brother holding his hand, as if unwilling to let it go:—the father,—sad moment! with a firm look, covering a prophetic sentiment, 'that all will not go well with his child,'—approaching to embrace him and bid him adieu.—Poor inconsiderate youth! From whose arms art thou flying? From what a shelter art thou going forth into a storm? Art thou weary of a father's affection, of a father's care? or, Hopest thou to find a warmer interest, a truer counsellor, or a kinder friend in a land of strangers, where youth is made a prey, and so many thousands are confederated to deceive them, and live by their spoils?

We will seek no farther than this idea, for the extravagancies by which the prodigal son added one unhappy example to the number: his fortune wasted,—the followers of it fled in course,—the wants of nature remain,—the hand of GOD gone forth against him,—'for when he had spent all, a mightly famine arose in that country.'— Heaven! have pity upon the youth, for he is in hunger and distress,— stray'd out of the reach of a parent, who counts every hour of his absence with anguish,—cut off from all his tender offices, by his folly,—and from relief and charity from others, by the calamity of the times.—

Nothing so powerfully calls home the mind as distress: the

tense fibre then relaxes,—the soul retires to itself,—sits pensive and susceptible of right impressions: if we have a friend, 'tis then we think of him; if a benefactor, at that moment all his kindnesses press upon our mind.—Gracious and bountiful GOD! Is it not for this that they who in their prosperity forget thee, do yet remember and return to thee in the hour of their sorrow? When our heart is in heaviness, upon whom can we think but thee, who knowest our necessities afar off,—puttest all our tears in thy bottle,—seest every careful thought,—hearst every sigh and melancholy groan we utter.—

Strange!—that we should only begin to think of GOD with comfort, when with joy and comfort we can think of nothing else.

Man surely is a compound of riddles and contradictions: by the law of his nature he avoids pain, and yet *unless he suffers in the flesh, he will not cease from sin,*[1] tho' it is sure to bring pain and misery upon his head for ever.

Whilst all went pleasurably on with the prodigal, we hear not one word concerning his father—no pang of remorse for the sufferings in which he had left him, or resolution of returning, to make up the account of his folly: his first hour of distress, seem'd to be his first hour of wisdom:—*When he came to himself, he said, How many hired servants of my father have bread enough to spare, whilst I perish!*—

Of all the terrors of nature, that of one day or another dying by hunger, is the greatest, and it is wisely wove into our frame to awaken man to industry, and call forth his talents; and though we seem to go carelessly, sporting with it as we do with other terrors—yet, he that sees this enemy fairly, and in his most frightful shape, will need no long remonstrance, to make him turn out of the way to avoid him.

It was the case of the prodigal—he arose to go to his father.—

—Alas! How shall he tell his story? Ye who have trod this round, tell me in what words he shall give in to his father, the sad *Items* of his extravagance and folly?

—The feasts and banquets which he gave to whole cities in the east,—the costs of Asiatic rarities,—and of Asiatic cooks to dress them,—the expences of singing men and singing women,—the

[1] reference to I *Peter* IV, 1 '. . . for he that hath suffered in the flesh hath ceased from sin . . .'

96

flute, the harp, the sackbut, and of all kinds of musick—the dress of the Persian courts, how magnificent! their slaves how numerous!—their chariots, their horses, their palaces, their furniture, what immense sums they had devoured!—what expectations from strangers of condition! what exactions!

How shall the youth make his father comprehend, that he was cheated at Damascus by one of the best men in the world;—that he lent a part of his substance to a friend at Nineveh, who had fled off with it to the Ganges;—that a whore of Babylon had swallowed his best pearl, and anointed the whole city with his balm of Gilead;—that he had been sold by a man of honour for twenty shekels of silver, to a worker in graven images;—that the images he had purchased had profited him nothing;—that they could not be transported across the wilderness, and had been burnt with fire at Shusan;—that the *apes and peacocks, which he had sent for from Tharsis, lay dead upon his hands; and that the mummies had not been dead long enough, which had brought him out of Egypt:—that all had gone wrong since the day he forsook his father's house.

—Leave the story—it will be told more concisely.—*When he was yet afar off, his father saw him,*—Compassion told it in three words—*he fell upon his neck and kissed him.*

Great is the power of eloquence: but never is it so great as when it pleads along with nature, and the culprit is a child strayed from his duty, and returned to it again with tears: Casuists may settle the point as they will: But what could a parent see more in the account, than the natural one, of an ingenuous heart too open for the world,—smitten with strong sensations of pleasures, and suffered to sally forth unarm'd into the midst of enemies stronger than himself?

Generosity sorrows as much for the overmatched, as Pity herself does.

The idea of a son so ruin'd, would double the father's caresses: every effusion of his tenderness would add bitterness to his son's remorse.—'Gracious Heaven! what a father I have rendered miserable!'

And he said, I have sinned against heaven, and in thy sight, and am no more worthy to be called thy son.

* Vide 2 *Chronicle* IX, 21.

But the father said, Bring forth the best robe.—

O ye affections! How fondly do you play at cross purposes with each other?—'Tis the natural dialogue of true transport: joy is not methodical; and where an offender, beloved, overcharges itself in the offence,—words are too cold; and a conciliated heart replies by tokens of esteem.

And he said unto his servants, Bring forth the best robe, and put it on him; and put a ring on his hand, and shoes on his feet, and bring hither the fatted calf, and let us eat and drink and be merry.

When the affections so kindly break loose, Joy, is another name for Religion.

We look up as we taste it: the cold Stoick without, when he hears the dancing and the music, may ask sullenly (with the elder brother) What it means, and refuse to enter: but the humane and compassionate all fly impetuously to the banquet, given *for a son who was dead and is alive again—who was lost and is found*. Gentle spirits, light up the pavilion with a sacred fire; and parental love, and filial piety lead in the mask with riot and festivity!—Was it not for this that GOD gave man music to strike upon the kindly passions; that nature taught the feet to dance to its movements, and as chief governess of the feast, poured forth wine into the goblet, to crown it with gladness?

The intention of this parable is so clear from the occasion of it, that it will not be necessary to perplex it with any tedious explanation: it was designed by way of indirect remonstrance to the Scribes and Pharisees, who animadverted upon our SAVIOUR's conduct, for entering so freely into conferences with sinners, in order to reclaim them. To that end, he proposes the parable of the shepherd, who left his ninety and nine sheep that were safe in the fold, to go and seek for one sheep that was gone astray,—telling them in other places, that they who were whole wanted not a physician,—but they that were sick:—and here, to carry on the same lesson, and to prove how acceptable such a recovery was to GOD, he relates this account of the prodigal son and his welcome reception.

I know not whether it would be a subject of much edification to convince you here, that our SAVIOUR, by the prodigal son, particularly pointed to those who were *sinners of the Gentiles*, and were recovered by divine Grace to repentance;—and that by the elder brother, he intended as manifestly the more froward of the Jews, who envied their conversion, and thought it a kind of wrong to their primogeniture, in being made fellow-heirs with them to the promises of GOD.

These uses have been so ably set forth, in so many good sermons upon the prodigal son, that I shall turn aside from them at present, and content myself with some reflections upon that fatal passion which led him,—and so many thousands after the example, *to gather all he had together, and take his journey into a far country.*

The love of variety, or curiosity of seeing new things, which is the same, or at least a sister passion to it,—seems wove into the frame of every son and daughter of Adam; we usually speak of it as one of nature's levities, tho' planted within us for the solid purposes of carrying forwards the mind to fresh inquiry and knowledge: strip us of it, the mind (I fear) would doze forever over the present page; and we should all of us rest at ease with such objects as presented themselves in the parish or province where we first drew breath.

It is to this spur which is ever in our sides, that we owe the impatience of this desire for travelling: the passion is no way bad,— but as others are,—in its mismanagement or excess;—order it rightly the advantages are worth the pursuit; the chief of which are —to learn the languages, the laws and customs, and understand the government and interest of other nations,—to acquire an urbanity and confidence of behaviour, and fit the mind more easily for conversation and discourse;—to take us out of the company of our aunts and grandmothers, and from the track of nursery mistakes; and by shewing us new objects, or old ones in new lights, to reform our judgements—by tasting perpetually the varieties of nature, to know what *is good*—by observing the address and arts of men, to conceive what *is sincere*—and by seeing the difference of so many humours and manners,—to look into ourselves and form our own.

This is some part of the cargo we might return with; but the impulse of seeing new sights, augmented with that of getting clear from all lessons both of wisdom and reproof at home—carries our youth too early out, to turn this venture too much to account; on the contrary, if the scene painted of the prodigal in his travels, looks more like a copy than an original,—will it not be well if such an adventurer, with so unpromising a setting out,—without *carte*,—without compass,—be not cast away for ever,—and may he not be said to escape well—if he returns to his country, only as naked, as he first left it?

But you will send an able pilot with your son—a scholar.—

If wisdom can speak in no other language but Greek or Latin,—you do well—or if mathematicks will make a man a gentleman,—or natural philosophy but teach him to make a bow,—he may be of some service in introducing your son into good societies, and supporting him in them when he has done—but the upshot will be generally this, that in the most pressing occasions of address,—if he is a man of reading, the unhappy youth will have the tutor to carry,—and not the tutor to carry him.

But you will avoid this extreme; he shall be escorted by one who knows the world, not merely from books—but from his own experience:—a man who has been employed on such services, and thrice made *the tour of Europe, with success.*

—That is, without breaking his own, or his pupil's neck;—for if he is such as my eyes have seen! some broken *Swiss valet de chambre,*—some general undertaker, who will perform the journey in so many months, 'IF GOD PERMIT,'—much knowledge will not accrue;—some profit at least,—he will learn the amount to a halfpenny, of every stage from Calais to Rome;—he will be carried to the best inns,—instructed where is the best wine, and sup a livre cheaper, than if the youth had been left to make the tour and bargain himself.—Look at our governor! I beseech you:—see, he is an inch taller, as he relates the advantages.—

—And here endeth his pride—his knowledge, and his use.

But when your son gets abroad, he will be taken out of his hand, by his society with men of rank and letters, with whom he will pass the greatest part of his time.

Let me observe in the first place,—that company which is really good, is very rare—and very shy: but you have surmounted this difficulty; and procured him the best letters of recommendation to the most eminent and respectable in every capital.—

And I answer, that he will obtain all by them, which courtesy strictly stands obliged to pay on such occasions,—but no more.

There is nothing in which we are so much deceived, as in the advantages proposed from our connexions and discourse with the literati, &c. in foreign parts; especially if the experiment is made before we are matured by years or study.

Conversation is a traffick; and if you enter into it, without some stock of knowledge, to ballance the account perpetually betwixt you, —the trade drops at once: and this is the reason,—however it may be boasted to the contrary, why travellers have little (especially good) conversation with the natives,—owing to their suspicion,— or perhaps conviction, that there is nothing to be extracted from the conversation of young itinerants, worth the trouble of their bad language,—or the interruption of their visits.

The pain on these occasions is usually reciprocal; the consequence of which is, that the disappointed youth seeks an easier society; and as bad company is always ready,—and ever lying in wait,— the career is soon finished; and the poor prodigal returns the same object of pity, with the prodigal in the Gospel.

Sermon XXIII
THE PARABLE OF THE RICH MAN
AND LAZARUS CONSIDERED[1]

Luke XVI. 31.

And he said unto him, If they hear not Moses and the prophets, neither will they be persuaded, tho' one should rise from the dead.

THESE WORDS are the conclusion of the parable of the rich man and Lazarus; the design of which was to shew us the necessity of conducting ourselves, by such lights as GOD had been pleased to give us: the sense and meaning of the patriarch's final determination in the text being this, That they who will not be persuaded to answer the great purposes of their being, upon such arguments as are offered to them in scripture, will never be persuaded to it by any other means, how extraordinary soever;—*If they hear not Moses and the prophets, neither will they be persuaded, though one should rise from the dead.*—

—Rise from the dead! To what purpose? What could such a messinger propose or urge, which had not been proposed and urged already? the novelty or surprise of such a visit might awaken the attention of a curious unthinking people, who spent their time in nothing else, but to hear and tell some new thing; but ere the wonder was well over, some new wonder would start up in its room, and then the man might return to the dead from whence he came, and not a soul make one enquiry about him.

—This, I fear, would be the conclusion of the affair. But to

[1] Sermon VIII in Vol. IV.

bring this matter still closer to us, let us imagine, if there is nothing unworthy in it, that GOD in compliance with a curious world,—or from a better motive,—in compassion to a sinful one, should vouchsafe to send one from the dead, to call home our conscience and make us better Christians, better citizens, better men, and better servants to GOD than what we are.

Now bear with me, I beseech you, in framing such an address, as I imagine, would be most likely to gain our attention, and conciliate the heart to what he had to say: the great channel to it, is Interest,—and there he would set out.

He might tell us, (after the most indisputable credentials of whom he served) That he was come a messenger from the great GOD of Heaven, with reiterated proposals, whereby much was to be granted us on his side,—and something to be parted with on ours: but, that, not to alarm us,—'twas neither houses, nor land, nor possessions;—'twas neither wives or children, or brethren, or sisters, which we had to forsake;—no one rational pleasure to be given up;—no natural endearment to be torn from—

—In a word, he would tell us, We had nothing to part with—but what was not in our interests to keep,—and that was our Vices; which brought death and misery to our doors.

He would go on, and prove it by a thousand arguments, that to be temperate and chaste, and just and peaceable, and charitable and kind to one another,—was only doing that for CHRIST's sake, which was most for our own; and that were we in a capacity of capitulating with GOD upon what terms we would submit to his government,—he would convince us, 'twould be impossible for the wit of man, to frame any proposals more for our present interests, than *to lead an uncorrupted life—to do the thing which is lawful and right,* and lay such restraints upon our appetites as are for the honour of human nature, and the refinement of human happiness.

When this point was made out, and the alarms from Interest got over,—the spectre might address himself to the other passions,—in doing this, he could but give us the most engaging ideas of the perfections of GOD,—or could he do more, than impress the most aweful ones, of his majesty and power:—he might remind us, that we are creatures but of a day, hastening to the place from whence we shall not return;—that during our stay, we stood accountable to this Being, who tho' rich in mercies,—yet was terrible in his judgements,—that he took notice of all our actions;—that he was about our paths, and about our beds, and spied out all our ways; and was so pure in his nature, that he would punish even the wicked imaginations of the heart, and had appointed a day, wherein he would enter into this inquiry.—

He might add—

But what?—with all the eloquence of an inspired tongue, What could he add or say to us, which had not been said before? the experiment has been tried a thousand times upon the hopes and fears, the reasons and passions of men, by all the powers of nature,—the application of which have been so great, and the variety of addresses so unanswerable, that there is not a greater paradox in the world, than that so good a religion should be no better recommended by its professors.

The fact is, mankind are not always in a humour to be convinced, —and so long as the pre-engagement with our passions subsists, it is not argumentation which can do the business;—we may amuse ourselves with the ceremony of the operation, but we reason not with the proper faculty, when we see every thing in the shape and colouring, in which the treachery of the senses paints it: and indeed, were we only to look into the world, and observe how inclinable men are to defend evil, as well as to commit it,—one would think, at first sight, they believed, that all discourses of religion and virtue were mere matters of speculation, for men to entertain some idle hours with; and conclude very naturally, that we seemed to be agreed in no one thing, but speaking well—and acting ill. But the truest comment is in the text,—*If they hear not Moses and the prophets*, &c.

If they are not brought over to the interests of religion upon such discoveries as GOD has made—or has enabled them to make, they will stand out against all evidence:—in vain shall *one* rise for their conviction;—was the earth to give up her dead—'twould be the same;—every man would return again to his course, and the same bad passions would produce the same bad actions to the end of the world.

This is the principal lesson of the parable; but I must enlarge upon the whole of it—because it has some other useful lessons, and they will best present themselves to us as we go along.

In this parable, which is one of the most remarkable in the gospel, our Saviour represents a scene, in which, by a kind of contrast, two of the most opposite conditions that could be brought together from human life, are pass'd before our imaginations.

The one, a man exalted above the level of mankind, to the highest pinnacle of prosperity,—to riches—to happiness—I say, *happiness*,— in compliance with the world, and on a supposition, that the possession of riches must make us happy, when the very pursuit of them so warms our imaginations that we stake both body and soul upon the event, as if they were things not to be purchased at too dear a rate. They are the wages of wisdom,—as well as of folly.—Whatever was the case here, is beyond the purport of the parable;—the scripture is silent, and so should we; it marks only his outward condition, by the common appendages of it, in the two great articles of Vanity and Appetite:—to gratify the one, he was cloathed in purple and fine linen: to satisfy the other,—fared sumptuously every day; —and upon every thing too—we'll suppose, that climates would furnish—that luxury could invent, or the hand of science could torture.

Close by his gates is represented the object whom Providence might seem to have placed there, to cure the pride of man, and shew him to what wretchedness his condition might be brought: a creature in all the shipwreck of nature,—helpless,—undone,—in want of friends, in want of health,—and in want of every thing with them which his distresses called for.

In this state he is described as desiring to be fed with the crumbs which fell from the rich man's table; and though the case is not expressly put, that he was refused, yet as the contrary is not affirmed in the historical part of the parable,—or pleaded after by the other, that he shewed mercy to the miserable, we may conclude his request was unsuccessful—like too many others in the world, either so high lifted up in it, that they cannot look down distinctly enough upon the sufferings of their fellow creatures,—or by long forfeiting in a continual course of banqueting and good cheer, they forget there is such a distemper as hunger, in the catalogue of human infirmities.

Overcharged with this, and perhaps, a thousand unpitied wants in a pilgrimage through an inhospitable world, the poor man sinks silently under his burden.—But good GOD! whence is this? Why doest thou suffer these hardships in a world which thou hast made? Is it for thy honour, that one man should eat the bread of fulness, and so many of his own stock and lineage eat the bread of sorrow?— That this man should go clad in purple, and have all his paths strewed with rosebuds of delight, whilst so many mournful passengers go heavily along, and pass by his gates, hanging down their heads? Is it for thy Glory, O GOD! that so large a shade of misery should be spread across thy works?—or, Is it that we see but a part of them? When the great chain at length is let down, and all that has held the two worlds in harmony is seen;—when the dawn of that day approaches, in which all the distressful incidents of this drama shall be unravel'd;—when every man's case shall be reconsidered,— then wilt thou be fully justified in all thy ways, and every mouth shall be stopped.

After a long day of mercy, mispent in riot and uncharitableness, the rich man *died also*:—the parable adds,—and was buried:— Buried no doubt in triumph, with all the ill-timed pride of funerals, and empty decorations, which worldly folly is apt to prostitute upon those occasions.

But this was the last vain show; the utter conclusion of all his epicurean grandeur;—the next is a scene of horror, where he is represented by our SAVIOUR, in a state of utmost misery, from whence he is supposed to lift up his eyes towards heaven, and cry to the patriarch Abraham for mercy.

And Abraham said, Son, remember that thou in thy lifetime receivedst thy good things.

—That he had received his good things,—'twas from heaven,— and could be no reproach: with what severity soever the scripture speaks against riches, it does not appear, that the living or faring sumptuously every day, was the crime objected to the rich man; or that it is a real part of a vicious character: the case might be then, as now: his quality and station in the world might have been supposed to be such, as not only to have justified his doing this, but, in general, to have required it without any imputation of doing wrong; for differences of stations there must be in the world, which must be supported by such marks of distinction as custom imposes. The exceeding great plenty and magnificence, in which Solomon is described to have lived, who had ten fat oxen, and twenty oxen out of the pastures, and a hundred sheep, besides harts and roebucks, and fallow deer and fatted fowl, with thirty measures of fine flour, and threescore measures of meal, for the daily provision of his table;[1]—all this is not laid to him as a sin, but rather remarked as an instance of GOD's blessing to him;—and whenever these things are otherwise, 'tis from a wasteful and dishonest perversion of them to pernicious ends,—and oft times, to the very opposite ones for which they were granted,—to glad the heart, to open it, and render it more kind.—

And this seems to have been the snare the rich man had fallen into—and possibly, had he fared less sumptuously,—he might have had more cool hours for reflection, and been better disposed to have conceived an idea of want, and to have felt compassion for it.

And Abraham said, Son, remember that thou in thy life time receivedst thy good things, and likewise Lazarus evil things.—Remember! sad subject of recollection! that a man has passed through this world with all the blessings and advantages of it, on his side,—favoured by GOD Almighty with riches,—befriended by his fellow creatures in the means of acquiring them,—assisted every hour by the society of which he is a member, in the enjoyment of them—to remember, how much he has received,—how little he has bestowed, —that he has been no man's friend,—no one's protector,—no one's benefactor,—blessed GOD!—

Thus begging in vain for himself, he is represented at last as interceding for his brethren, that Lazarus might be sent to them to give them warning, and save them from the ruin which he had fallen into;—*They have Moses and the prophets*, was the answer of the patriarch,—*let them hear them*; but the unhappy man is represented, as discontented with it; and still persisting in his request, and urging,—*Nay, father Abraham, but if one went from the dead, they would repent.*

—He thought so—but Abraham knew otherwise:—And the grounds of the determination, I have explained already,—so shall proceed to draw some other conclusions and lessons from the parable.

And first, our SAVIOUR might further intend to discover to us

[1] I *Kings* IV, 22.

by it, the dangers to which great riches naturally expose mankind, agreeably to what is elsewhere declared, how hardly shall they who have them, enter the kingdom of Heaven.

The truth is, they are often too dangerous a blessing for GOD to trust us with, or we to manage: they surround us at all times with ease, with nonsense, with flattery, and false friends, with which thousands and ten thousands have perished:—they are apt to multiply our faults, and treacherously to conceal them from us;—they hourly administer to our temptations;—and allow us neither time to examine our faults, or humility to repent them:—nay, what is strange, do they not often tempt men even to covetousness; and tho' amidst all the ill offices which riches do us, one would last suspect this vice, but rather think the one a cure for the other; yet so it is, that many a man contracts his spirits upon the enlargement of his fortune, and is the more empty for being full.

But there is less need to preach against this: we seem all to be hastening to the opposite extreme of luxury and expense: we generally content ourselves with the solution of it; and say, 'Tis a natural consequence of trade and riches—and there it ends.

By the way, I affirm, there is a mistake in the account; and that it is not riches which are the cause of luxury,—but the corrupt calculation of the world, in making riches the balance for honour, for virtue, and for every thing that is great and good, which goads so many thousands on with an affectation of possessing more than they have,—and consequently engaging in a system of expences they cannot support.

In one word, 'tis the necessity of *appearing* to be somebody, in order to be so—which ruins the world.

This leads us to another lesson in the parable, concerning the true use and application of riches; we may be sure from the treatment of the rich man, that he did not employ those talents as GOD intended.—

How GOD did intend them,—may as well be known from an appeal to your own hearts, and the inscription you shall read there, —as from any chapter and verse I might cite on the subject. Let us then for a moment, my dear auditors! turn our eyes that way, and consider the traces which even the most insensible man may have proof of, from what he may perceive springing up within him from some casual act of generosity; and tho' this is a pleasure which properly belongs to the good, yet let him try the experiment;—let him comfort the captive, or cover the naked with a garment, and he will feel what is meant by that moral delight arising in the mind from the conscience of a humane action.

But to know it right, we must call upon the compassionate;—Cruelty gives evidence unwillingly, and feels the pleasure but imperfectly; for this, like all other pleasures, is of a relative nature, and consequently the enjoyment of it, requires some qualification in the faculty, as much as the enjoyment of any other good does:—there must be something antecedent in the disposition and temper which will render that good,—a good to that individual; otherwise, though 'tis true it may be possessed,—yet it never can be enjoyed.

Consider how difficult you will find it to convince a miserly heart, that any thing is good, which is not profitable? or a libertine one, that any thing is bad, which is pleasant?

Preach to a voluptuary, who has modell'd both mind and body to no other happiness but good eating and drinking,—bid him *taste and see how good God is*:[1]—there is not an invitation in all nature would confound him like it.

In a word, a man's mind must be like your proposition before it can be relished; and 'tis the resemblance between them, which brings over his judgement, and makes him an evidence on your side.

'Tis therefore not to the cruel,—'tis to the merciful;—to those who rejoice with those that rejoice, and weep with them that weep, —that we make this appeal:—'tis to the generous, the kind, the humane, that I am now to tell the sad* story of the fatherless, and of him who hath no helper, and bespeak your almsgiving in behalf of those, who know not how to ask for it themselves.

—What can I say more?—it is a subject on which I cannot inform your judgement,—and in such an audience, I would not presume to practise upon your passions: let it suffice to say, that they whom GOD hath blessed with the means,—and for whom he has done more, in blessing them likewise with disposition;—have abundant reason to be thankful to him, as the author of every good

[1] from Psalm 34, 8.

* Charity sermon at St. Andrew's, Holborn (delivered 3 May, 1761. ed.).

gift, for the measure he hath bestowed to them of both: 'tis the refuge against the stormy wind and tempest, which he has planted in our hearts; and the constant fluctuation of every thing in this world, forces all the sons and daughters of Adam to seek shelter under it by turns. Guard it by entails and settlements as we will, the most affluent plenty may be stripp'd, and find all its worldly comforts like so many withered leaves dropping from us;—the crowns of princes may be shaken; and the greatest that ever awed the world, have looked back and moralized upon the turn of the wheel.

That which has happened to one,—may happen to every man; and therefore that excellent rule of our SAVIOUR, in acts of benevolence, as well as every thing else, should govern us;—*that whatsoever ye would that men should do to you, do ye also unto them.*

Hast thou ever laid upon the bed of languishing, or laboured under a distemper which threatened thy life? Call to mind thy sorrowful and pensive spirit at that time, and say, What it was that made the thoughts of death so bitter:—if thou hast children,—I affirm it, the bitterness of death lay there;—if unbrought up, and unprovided for, What will become of them? Where will they find a friend when I am gone, who will stand up for them, and plead their cause against the wicked?

—Blessed GOD! to thee, who art a father to the fatherless, and a husband to the widow,—I entrust them.

Hast thou ever sustained any considerable shock in thy fortune? or, Has the scantiness of thy condition hurried thee into great straits, and brought thee almost to distraction? Consider what was it that spread a table in that wilderness of thought,—who made thy cup overflow? Was it not a friend of consolation who stepped in,—saw thee embarrassed with tender pledges of thy love, and the partner of thy cares,—took them under his protection?—Heaven! thou wilt reward him for it!—and freed thee from all the terrifying apprehensions of a parent's love.

—Hast thou—

—But how shall I ask a question which must bring tears to so many eyes?—Hast thou ever been wounded in a more affecting manner still, by the loss of a most obliging friend,—or been torn away from the embraces of a dear and promising child by the stroke of death?—bitter remembrance! nature droops at it—but nature is the same in all conditions and lots in life.—A child thrust forth in an evil hour, without food, without raiment, bereft of instruction, and the means of salvation, is a subject of most tender heart-aches, and will awaken every power of nature:—as we have felt for ourselves,—let us feel for CHRIST's sake—let us feel for theirs: and may the GOD of all comfort bless you. Amen.